Out of  the Prayer Book

Volume 1

Prayers from My Journal

Mike Freed

First Edition

R. Michael Freed

Wichita, KS

Independently Published

Scripture quotations marked (WEB) are from the World English Bible and are a part of the Public Domain

Book Layout © 2017 BookDesignTemplates.com

Library of Congress Control Number: 2024900418

Out of the Lunchbox - Volume 1/ Mike Freed. -- 1st ed.
ISBN 9798858743521

Independently Published

To my granddaughters, Karlie and Maddie and to generations yet unborn, may you continue to learn of and share the tremendous love of God in Jesus! Keep the Faith! Trust and hope only in Him!

CONTENTS

Introduction

Jesus therefore lifting up his eyes, and seeing that a great multitude was coming to him, said to Philip, "Where are we to buy bread, that these may eat?" He said this to test him, for he himself knew what he would do.

Philip answered him, "Two hundred denarii worth of bread is not sufficient for them, that every one of them may receive a little."

One of his disciples, Andrew, Simon Peter's brother, said to him, "There is a boy here who has five barley loaves and two fish, but what are these among so many?" (John 6:5-9 WEB)

Jesus' feeding of the 5000 is one of my favorite Bible stories. It is recorded in all four gospels, but only John's account includes the detail that it was a boy that had the five loaves and two fish that started it all.

I picture the lad tugging on Andrews clothes and pestering him saying, "I have some food! Jesus can have it! Tell him! Tell him!" and continuing persistently, until reluctantly Andrew speaks up half-heartedly and says, "There is a boy here who has five barley loaves and two fish, but what are these among so many?" Little did they know the miracle that Jesus would perform.

I have not always been as anxious and excited as that boy to share the things I have, things which God has given me in the first place, but I am learning to offer them back to God and ask his blessing upon them.

All of us are called to share what we have with others, whether small or large. We are called to ask God to bless them, multiply them and use them as he sees fit. One of the things I have been "given" over the years are volumes and volumes of journal entries, a "Lunchbox" if you will, mostly of prayers. These journal entries still feed me, as I reread a few each day.

First and foremost, these entries remind me of what a great, merciful, and praiseworthy God we have! They also remind me of things in my life that I need God's help with, changes I wish to make, the person I am with the Spirit's help becoming, the progress I am making and much more.

For a long time, I kept my writings to myself. Then one day it occurred to me that if what I had written was helpful to me, then perhaps it might be helpful to others as well. So, I decided. not without some trepidation, that it was time to "Open the Lunchbox" and share my "Fish and Bread" with the world, asking Jesus to use it, bless it, and multiply it as he sees fit.

My first effort to share some of what I had written was a book entitled "Drummer Boy's Lunchbox." It was a smorgasbord of Bible passages, original poems, prayers, stories, questions, and other writings woven together with narrative written specifically for the book and illustrated in part by my granddaughter who was 9 at the time.

In keeping with the original theme, I have titled this work "Out of the Lunchbox," though the format is much simpler. I have just taken several of what I considered helpful prayers from my journals, removed some of the more mundane, everyday details, cleaned up punctuation, spelling, and grammar a bit (but just a little) and published them.

You won't find perfection here! For the most part the entries are as I wrote them. The only changes I have made were simply to make them a little more presentable and readable than they originally occurred in my journal.

My journaling process is that I free write pretty much whatever comes to mind, rapidly and without stopping to judge, rewrite or correct anything. I am sometimes amazed at what comes out. Over the years I have developed the habit of recounting to my heavenly Father, Dad, Abba, the events of the past day before launching into praise, thanksgiving, and requests. It is mostly these daily recaps that I have removed.

I believe God, who numbers even the hairs on our heads, is interested in the day-to-day events and happenings in our lives and it is helpful to me, especially as I age, in remembering things that have happened. I didn't feel, however, that the drama and details of these daily accounts would be helpful to you, the reader, and so have usually removed them.

You will find many recurring words, phrases, and themes in these prayers. Some of these are from favorite sections of scriptures or liturgy that are finding their way into my being and soul. I have included the references to some of them in the section entitled, Bible Passages.

Many of my prayers contain expressions of thanksgiving and praise. And while I'm sure God likes to hear them; I have found that coming to God in gratitude and adoration has profoundly changed me for the better in the process, as I remind myself daily of his goodness, mercy, and love!

Likewise, you will find recurring request for God to help me make changes in my life. Change often takes time, sometimes I am a slow learner, and scripture encourages us to be persistent in prayer!

Often my prayers can be long and rambling. I do not consider this a model for prayer necessarily. God does not hear us because of our many words. I think that is just my style, part of my personality and contributed to by the fact that I have a bipolar disorder and sometimes get a little manic and wordy in the process.

I often write and pray in phrases and run-on sentences with little or no punctuation. To make things more readable, yet preserve the original style and flavor, I have often broken up and punctuated these with explanation points. This propensity to use explanation points is sometimes just a matter of convenience, but more often it also helps to convey the sense of urgency, excitement, or enthusiasm in the original. I use explanation points much the way Mark used the word, "immediately" in his gospel. (At least that's my rationalization!)

Sometimes I simply string things together using "ands." I have cleaned up some of these "run-on ands" with commas and fewer conjunctions, but just as often I have left them as written, for no particular reason.

These prayers were written over several years, and I was at different places in my life at different times. Consequently, you may see contradictory and conflicting ideas at times. Like Elijah, David, and others in scripture, I have also experienced periods of doubt, questioning and depression that sometimes colored my prayers. I believe God wants us to be honest and authentic in our prayers and to share with Him the full range of our questions, feelings, and emotions. I hope this is reflected in these prayers.

These prayers are not ment to be models or examples of how to pray. They are simply the proclamations and declarations of my heart and mind. My hope and prayer for you is that they are helpful to you in finding your own unique and authentic expressions of prayer, whether spoken or written.

These prayers are arranged pretty much in the order in which I retrieved them from my journals. The prayer titles are usually a few words that jumped out at me from the prayer and may or may not capture the essence of the prayer. The titles were just a convenient way to give some sense of order to the book and perhaps spur interest in reading a particular prayer. Feel free to read them in whatever order seems helpful.

I often address God as "Dad" or even "daddy," as these were the ways I most often addressed my earthly father and I believe that God wants us to come to Him as his little children. If these are too informal or uncomfortable for you, simply use the form of address that you are comfortable with.

More and more I have begun to use the Aramaic/Biblical word for Father, Abba as I address God. I also sometimes use the transliterated Hebrew name for God, Yahweh, or YHWH and for Jesus, Yeshua. The meanings of these words are difficult to track down. We do not even know exactly how they were pronounced.

YHWH seems to be related to the words for "I Am" (See the story of Moses and the burning bush). The name was held in such high regard that when it was read aloud, the word Adonai was usually substituted or as many English versions translate it, The LORD.

Yeshua has as its root(s) the word for "save" or "salvation" or some would say "God" or "Yahweh Saves!" I am not a Hebrew scholar and have but a passing knowledge of all this. If you wish to know more, please consult someone more qualified than myself.

There are many ways you could use this book but let me suggest one. First read a section of Scripture. There are many good ones in the section of this book entitled Bible Passages or use one of your own choosing. Second read a prayer from my journal. Finaly, write whatever comes to your heart and mind in your own journal. This may be a paper book, a word processing document or one of the many journalling apps available, both free and paid. I currently use Diarium and find it helpful.

I have found free writing, writing quickly whatever comes to mind without stopping to think or judge it, helpful. You may wish to write more thoughtfully and intentionally. Make it your own and review your entries from time to time.

Finally, you may notice that this book is published in a larger font than many. When I finished my first book, my wife, who has some vision issues, informed me that the print was too small. So, in this book I am using mostly a 14-point font, which hopefully will be a helpful compromise between normal sized print and what would officially be considered large print.

Blessings, as you read and pray!

Prayers From My Journal

Thank-you!

Thank you, God, for today! Amen! (by Rebekah Freed at age 2 as recorded in my journal)

Oh, for a faith that rubs bare the print of scripture!

Dear Father

You are God of God! Great I Am! Yahweh of old! Source of all that exists! You made us and you re-deemed us in your Son, the holy one of Israel, set apart to die and rise for us, that we might appear before you, without fear!

We know not fully the substance or form of this man! Help us to not be ashamed of him but to embrace him as brother and savior and friend! Like us in every way, yet one with you, God with you and with the Spirit or so we have been taught!

But our minds buckle and fail when we try and comprehend you, oh God! So perhaps it is enough to say, "Our God is one!"

Make us one with you! Dear father of goodness and light and life! In my pride, I sometimes think I know more or have come further in my understanding than others and humility escapes me!

If I have seen more clearly, it is because I have "stood on the shoulders of giants!" Giants of faith, like my grandparents, Albert and Elsie! Oh, for a faith that rubs bare the print of scripture! Oh, for a faith that loves like Alberta and Linda! Oh, for the childlikeness of Karlie and Maddie!

Father God, I am humbled in your presence for you call me child and bride, brother, and friend! What love and mercy and forgiveness and patience you shower on me, on us! Let us not take it for granted but cherish it all our days!

Teach me to live humbly, yet boldly and courageously, not forgetting that I am a child of the king with privileges and responsibilities, with power and authority over evil forces! Help me to remember that all the resources of heaven and earth are at my disposal and that God the very creator of the universe dwells in me and around me and is with me, wherever I go! Let me not lose heart! Let me not fail or faint! Renew me by your presence when I grow weary! Uphold me with your right hand when I face adversity and difficulty!

You are a great God and Father, brother, savior, and friend, husband and mother and sister! Better and more faithful still than all of these! Oh, daddy God, come! Lord Jesus, come! Come, Holy Spirit Come! Come dear God and in your perfect timing, bring all things to their perfect end and a new beginning in you!

For you have said, "behold I make all things new!" Thy kingdom come! Thy will be done!

Amen and Amen and Amen! In Jesus name! Save us dear, Father-Yahweh! Amen!

Do miracles with the mundanc and make the miraculous common among us!

Dear Dad,

You are a great God and Father, a faithful brother and savior and friend! You breathe into us your good Spirit! You give us life and love! You give us light for our being.! You give plan and purpose and meaning to our existence. You number and order our days.

Teach us to order them aright. To be intentional about the things we do. To guard our motives and desires. Often, we do things with mixed motives. Purify our heart and mind. Give us the mind and heart and Spirit of your Son. Teach us to love and live and give and pray with pure hearts and minds, with pure motives of good intention. Thy kingdom come! Thy will be done!

Remove anxiety and fear far from us and fill us with a spirit of courage and hope, faith and love! Love us and lead us, by the hand and by the heart! Carry us, drag us kicking and screaming if you must but do not desert us, good Spirit of life and truth and love! Indwell us and change us and make us one! Be thou our hearts desire and delight! Teach us to open our eyes wide, to love with Christ's intention and abandon. To go to difficult places! To do difficult things for your sake and the sake of others! Thy kingdom come! Thy will be done! Love us lead us!

Sometimes Father, we need tough love and sometimes we need you to wrap your arms around us and rock us as your little child, to comfort us and assure us it will be alright! I dream dreams and see visions. Help me to bring them to fruition! If not me Father God, then someone else you have prepared for the task.

Let all the people praise you, let the mountains and the trees, the oceans and rivers and dry land sing your praises and tell of your great goodness and mercy and glory! Let all creation return to you the honor due and let it relish in your love and kindness! Let us love one another in peace and joy, in harmony and oneness of mind, body and Spirit! Let all the people praise You, in this dimension and the next, in time and space and in eternity that knows no bounds! Let all the people praise you! Love us! Lead us! Motivate and transform us into children of light and love and goodness and hope and faith.

We desire to do great things. Purify and refine and transform that desire. Sanctify the mundane and the miraculous. Do miracles with the mundane and make the miraculous common among us! Sanctify us; set us apart to be your children! Make us holy and righteous in you and in your son! Love us! Lead us! Cause us to pray, "Thy Kingdom come! Thy will be done!" and then transform us into agents and ambassadors of that coming! Love us! Lead us !

You are our God and Father, apart from you we don't even exist! We are branches to be burned; chaff to be blown away on the wind! We have no being of our own and when we turn to our own sinful intentions and desires, there is much weeping and gnashing of teeth, much fear and hatred and loneliness and despair!

But in you there is hope! In you there is new life! In you there is plan and purpose, joy and love and companionship and communion and oneness and hope! Love us! Lead Us! Transform us by the work of your good Spirit within us! Break down the walls that separate and divide and destroy and make us one! Call those who are far off and those who are near and sanctify us all in the body of your Son, our Lord and Savior, our brother and friend, even Jesus the Christ who lives and reigns with you! Love Us lead us! Cause us to dwell in harmony and love and oneness and faith and hope! Thy kingdom come! Thy will be done, in us and through us and round about us and among us!

Let your works and your ways be marvelous in our sight! Teach us to love in You! Teach us to hope in You! Teach us to trust in you! Teach us to do all things in you and in your name and the name of your son proclaiming, "Yahweh saves!" "Blessed be Yahweh, the great "I AM," our creator and redeemer and salvation and hope.

Lead us forth in love and courage and oneness of purpose! Let all the people praise You! From the greatest to the least let them sing songs of gladness, joy, love, and praise! Amen and Amen! In Jesus Name, Amen!

Imagination carries me away

Dear Dad,

Your Mercies are new every morning! Your loving kindness fills the sky! In your hands are the deep places of the earth and the tallest mountains reside in you! The moon, all the planets, and the stars are contained in your being. You set them in place by the words of your mouth and in you we live and move and have our being!

Great "I Am," who is like you spirit, and person! Three persons in one, who made all and contains all! You are incomprehensible beyond our imagination and yet you formed us in your image and delight in making us your children. I ramble and write of that which I know little; my imagination carries me away.

I praise and thank and expound upon what I cannot comprehend! Father God, let me find my life and purpose and being in you and in your Son! Move in me to make me perfect and righteous in your eyes, not righteous in and of myself, but clothed and wrapped and dwelling and being in your righteousness and in the righteousness of your Son.

Many things press in on me today! They seek to occupy my time in this place. Grant wisdom, discernment, love, hope, joy, and peace that I may live this day and everyday well in you.

I am so easily distracted by the mundane and meaningless things of this life. I get wrapped up in the trivial and the urgent. Help me to focus on you and on your people.

Father God, all things are in your keeping! Keep us and prosper us and make us a blessing this day and always! Abide with us and keep us! Dwell in us and transform our very being! Let rivers of light and life and love and forgiveness flow from us and enrich and transform the lives of others!

You have created us with a plan and a purpose! Lead us to live in that purpose! To live out that purpose for our benefit and the benefit of others! Let all that I do bring you glory and honor and praise!

Let all the people praise you, oh God! Let all the people praise you, from the greatest to the least, let them shout and sing of your great goodness and mercy! Let all the people praise you! In Jesus Name, Amen!

I distress myself often thinking or imagining the worst!

Dear Dad,

Still my anxious heart and help me to remember that you work all things out for good! Help me to take care of the things I need or am supposed to take care of and to let go of worry and anxiety and fear! Thy kingdom come! Thy will be done! Love us! Lead us!

You are light and life and love! I distress myself often thinking or imagining the worst! Forgive me! Let me hope in you! You delight in giving good things to your children! You want what's best for us! You have our best interest at heart! Thy kingdom come! Thy will be done! Love us and lead us and shalom us in your grace!

In Jesus Name, Amen and Amen!

Let us come to you as your little children!

Dear Dad,

You love us with relentless, passionate, tender, everlasting love! You are our God! You are our Father! You are our hearts desire and delight! In you do we hope! In you do we trust! Not in money or cars or homes or this world's goods, but in you!

You are the light of the world! You are grace and truth and hope and life! In you do we hope and pray! In you do we trust!

You restore youth and vitality, passion, and purpose! You give plan and purpose to our being! You are our all in all! We are content in you! Oh Father God, dear abba, dear daddy, let us come to you as your little children! Let us depend on you for life and livelihood! For food and drink and all good things!

You know our needs! Teach us to live simple lives of love and kindness, mercy and justice and peace! Teach us to live simple lives in you! Thy kingdom come! Thy will be done! Love us! Lead us!

Light of light and goodness, courage and strength, You are the light and life of the world! You are our light and life, our courage and passion and strength,

Often, we stumble and fall! Too often we turn from you to other things! Thy kingdom come! Thy will be done!

Turn our hearts back to you! Let our love and our light and life be in you! Show us the way to go! Show us the next step and give us courage and strength and desire and love to take it! You are our light and our salvation! You are our hope! In you do we live and move and have our being! In you, do the nations hope! Let our trust be in you! In you will we hope and trust! In Jesus Name, Amen!

All the superlatives in the world are not enough

Dear Dad,

You are a great God and Father! I am so grateful to have you in my life! You love us with an infinite, passionate, relentless, and jealous love! You want only the best for us! You are the best! In you do we live and move and have our being! In you do we find plan and purpose and being! You are our light and our life! You are our creator and sustainer! You cause us to survive and thrive! You make us new in the image and righteousness of your Son! You wash away all our sins and shortcomings! You remove them far from us! You remember them no more, nor do you count them against us!

Every day is fresh and new with you! You are the light and life of the world! You created us and all things! You carved out and formed time and space and dimensions beyond our knowing! You called them into being where nothing existed!

It boggles our minds! We struggle to comprehend your essence! To comprehend your great goodness and being! From everlasting to everlasting, you are God, the fount and source and sustainer of all things! You are goodness and light! You are love and mercy and justice! Your essence permeates and sustains the universe! Yet your good spirit deigns to inhabit our mortal bodies and give us life!

You teach us the way to go! You lead us down paths of love and kindness, generosity, forgiveness, goodness, and mercy! You are our light and our life! You are an ever-present help and guide!

Help us to hear and listen and follow your voice! Thy kingdom come! Thy will be done! Love us! Lead us!

Oh God, of truth and light, love and being, Father God, all the superlatives in the world are not enough to describe your goodness and mercy and love! We write to praise and honor you and your great name! We write to remind ourselves and others what a great God and Father you are! We go into this day proclaiming the name of Jesus! Saying, "Yahweh Saves!" "Blessed be the name of Yahweh, the great I am of all that exists! Amen and Amen! In Jesus Name, Amen!

Fill our days with the abundance of your mercy

Dear Dad,
Your mercies are new every morning! They rise with the dawn! The sleep of the night refreshes us and reminds us that we have another new day in you! Another day of grace and love and forgiveness! Teach us, good Father, for often we have gone astray and done things we have not really wanted to do. Lead us by the hand and carry us from our wayward places. Renew our hearts and minds and spirits! Give us light and life and love! Oneness of purpose hope and trust in you!

You are the great God and Father! You alone bring us salvation and light and love! Were it not for your grace, we would be without hope!

Change hearts and minds! Call us to true repentance and fullness of life! Call us to hope and to a plan and purpose in you! Our works and our ways are not our own, they are in your keeping! You number our days according to your great love and purpose!

Give us light and love and purpose and hope in you. Fill our days with the abundance of your mercy and make us vessels and agents to carry that love and mercy to others!

Thy word is truth and life, light and love! Fill us with the Spirit of your living word, the word made flesh among us! Father we are ignorant! We are as little children before you! Lead us, guide us! Teach us to love and hope and trust in you! Apart from you we can do nothing! Apart from you, we wither and die and are lost! In you, however, is life and hope! In you is the fullness of joy! Let your joy and your laughter be upon us and in us! Dwell in us and transform us into your children of light and love! In you there is fullness of life!

Let all the people praise you! Oh God, let all the people praise you! Let the fullness of the number of souls be complete and let them come to you with great thanks and praise! Though they may tremble at your coming, calm their fears and transform their hearts that they may praise you with laughing and dancing and singing.! That they may bring you an offering of un-ending thanksgiving and praise!

Let all the people praise you, from one generation to the next, in this dimension and the one to come! In ways and in numbers, in races and colors and sizes and shapes we can't even imagine, from the earth and from thousands upon thousands of planets yet unknown! Let every tribe and race bring you thanksgiving and praise! Let us praise and thank our God with our words and with our actions of love and kindness!

Let all the people praise you, on earth and in the heavens. God our God and our brother and redeemer, the lamb of God has saved us! Praise him all you, peo-ple! Bring him the thanks and praise, due his name! Amen and Amen! In Jesus Name Amen!

Sick and tired -Leave a legacy

Dear Dad,

I'm sick and tired of being, sick and tired, of being overweight and unhealthy. I'm sick and tired of being in debt and living paycheck to paycheck. I'm sick and tired of not living up to my full potential as your child! I'm sick and tired of being afraid! Afraid I might fail, afraid I might succeed, afraid of all the could-bes and might-bes! Afraid of leading others astray! Afraid of things becoming worse! Afraid of increased responsibilities! I'm sick and tired of not fully using the talents and abilities you have given me! I'm sick and tired of too often, taking the easy road, of shortcutting things and being afraid of hard work! I'm sick and tired of making excuses and settling for less!

Father God, you have been so generous and patient with me! I like to think that in some areas I've made progress. Slow progress, three-steps-forward-and-two steps-back-progress. The life I have now is a great life, but it could be so much better. I could be and do so much more than I currently am and do.

Father, protect me from pride and envy, protect me from despair and depression. Protect me from the grass-is-always-greener-syndrome. Free me, Father, to be and do all that you would have me be and do in you!

The living God dwells within me! The Spirit and power of Christ dwells within me and upon me and around me. Show me true abundance! Abundance of truth! Abundance of love and hope and joy! Abundance of faith and trust!

The thief would steal all those things from me, but you have come that I might have life and have it to the full, rich and overflowing abundant life.

I want to leave a legacy, a legacy of faith and trust in you and in your Son, our Savior, and brother, and friend! A legacy of love and relationship! A legacy of hope and joy and peace! A legacy of reconciliation and forgiveness! A legacy of courage! A legacy of never giving up and of trusting in you! A legacy of health in mind, body, and spirit! A legacy of wisdom! A legacy of health in financial matters! A legacy of generosity and gratitude! A legacy of kindness! A legacy of laughter and joy and hope! A legacy of hard work and honesty and character and of goodness, light, and love!

Father God, you did miracles with fish and bread. You did miracles with mud made from spital and dirt. You did miracles with touch and words, miracles with simple water. Do now miracles in me! Miracles with this earthen vessel! Miracles with this seed of life you have sown within me!

It is all gift! Help me to do the hard work that makes your gifts shine like the stars! Love me and lead me, even as you have done all the days of my life! Make thy way plain before me!

I know not what lies before me, whether humble things or great, my paths are in your keeping. Fill me with love and wisdom, determination, and hope! Fill me with gratitude!

Let my latter days far exceed my former! Work in me and through me! Do more than I can think or imagine! Use me to bring your salvation and life to many! Change worlds and dimensions beyond time and space! Things unknown to me! People yet unborn and tribes whose language I do not speak!

Father, my spirit carries me away to things I know nothing about! Things it is not wise for mortals to ponder!

Thy will be done! Thy kingdom come in me and through me and round about me! In the here and now and in the great beyond!

I cannot fathom your being! Your works and your ways are too marvelous for me! I am a mere babe in wisdom and knowledge, in love and trust and hope and joy!

Feed me, oh Spirit of life and love and truth! Feed me on the body and blood of my savior and friend, your son, my brother, the bread of life come down from heaven, the water of life, the living water that becomes a well springing up inside me unto eternal life! Love me and lead me! Dwell within me and walk beside me! Teach me to walk humbly with you, acknowledging you as God and Father, Savior and brother and friend, as fount and source of all I am and can do! To walk with gratitude and thankfulness and joy! Help me also to walk courageously with you, knowing that you are on my side, that the almighty God of the universe and all his resources are at my disposal!

Let me spread justice and mercy and love, hope, and joy, wherever I go! You are a great God and Father who does more than I can think or ask or even imagine! Thy will be done, in me and through me and round about me! In Jesus Name Amen and Amen!

Afraid to "pursue the lion."

Dear Dad,

Forgive me for my fears and for my unwillingness to trust you. Forgive me, for my pride and arrogance. I am a big dreamer, and yet I am afraid to "pursue the lion."

I wasted days and years asking again and again if my dreams and plans are from you! I have wasted too much time looking for easier or better ways to do things, rather than jumping in and getting dirty and getting it done! I talk a good game and sometimes (in some ways) I do pretty well as a player and in other ways I fall short!

Is it time to step up the game, or retire, or go into coaching. You told the Israelites to go into battle and they refused! Later they said they would go. They went in their own strength, and they were slaughtered. I don't want to go anywhere you are not with me. I want to follow your lead. Fight your battles and do what you would have me to do.

If I am to perish here and sojourn in the desert until my time is over then, so be it! Let me do it, knowing that you have indeed been with me and let me receive with joy and gladness and gratitude the manna you give day by day! And if instead, if you wish to restore me, if you wish to again place dreams and visions and plans in my life, then let me go in your strength and pursue them with the courage and boldness and faith that come from you!

Put mentors and teacher and coaches in my life that inspire and give good advice. Teach me to work hard and faithfully, day-by-day, and not to shortcut the process!

My days are in your keeping; bless them, multiply them, and use them for your good purpose! Thy kingdom come! Thy will be done! In Jesus Name, Amen!

Somedays, I wonder if I even know you

Father God, Dear Brother Jesus,

Somedays, I wonder if I even know you and other days your voice seems so clear and so strong!

I mourn over this world and the people in it. I mourn for myself and all your precious little ones. I just want to love people, including myself!

Sometimes what is put forth in the Bible is so condemning. I just want to know that you got my back! That you love me dearly, as I love my children and even more!

I don't understand love! I don't understand you or Jesus or even myself sometimes! Why can't we just get along?

Father God, Brother Jesus, not sure where I'm going with this. I just know I can't stay in the depressed mess I was in yesterday! Go with me or I perish! I have no light and no love within me, except what you have put there. Come life-giving Spirit and restore my hope and my joy in you! Be thou my joy and my light and my love! Be thou my sure hope! Be thou my Sunday School Jesus!

I'm crying again, Father God! Crying over just what I am not sure! Know me and grant that I may know you and love you with all my being! You are the God and Father that can do more than we can think or even imagine! Teach us to love and to live!

I'm tired of being afraid of you! I want to believe that you are the all-knowing all-wise and all-caring God, but sometimes you just seem like a fellow traveler in this journey of life. If so, I love you anyway! I need you in my life, Father God, brother Jesus! I love You guys! In Jesus Name!

In this is love, not that we loved God, but that he loved us, and sent his Son as the atoning sacrifice for our sins. Beloved, if God loved us in this way, we also ought to love one another. No one has seen God at any time. If we love one another, God remains in us, and his love has been perfected in us.
(1 John 4:10-12 WEB)

Form from me a vessel fit for your habitation

Father, you know my heart and you know my thoughts! You know that they are not always pure, but by the power of your good Spirit within me I do love you and I have changed for the better.

You are the way, the truth, and the life! Lead me back to the Father, dear brother of faith and truth and life! Purge me! Let me vomit up the last remaining evil within me! Let it be blown away as chaff. Let it be skimmed off or burned away as dross in molten Gold or Silver!

Form from me a vessel fit for your habitation and service! A living cup or bowl filled to overflowing with your love and your grace and your mercy! Let those gifts overflow in my life and enrich the lives of those around me!

My life is abundant and full because of your presence! You heal my infirmities! You lift me up as on eagle's wings! You renew my youth and I dream dreams and see visions of your everlasting love!

Father God, let my latter days exceed my former in loving and serving you and others! You are the God who keeps me even unto old age! My days are in your keeping of God! Whether few or many in this world is up to you!

You have known me, and you have searched me and often I have failed the test, yet you did not desert me! Oh God, you walked with me every step of the way! Often, I would not have made it had you not carried me! Father God, faithful savior and brother and friend, indwelling life giving, life altering Spirit, continue with me all the days of this life and by your grace receive me, in your proper timing, into the life that is to come! Bless now this day and those in it! Amen and Amen! In Jesus Name Amen!

Some days courage is the will to crawl out of bed.

Some days courage is the will to crawl out of bed and to start! To throw in a load of laundry! To type a few words on the keys! To begin the next thing on the list or to make a list!

Feeling beat down today, Father God, but at your word I will begin! At your word I will cast my net on the other side of the boat in hopes of a catch!

Grow my courage and my actions, Father God! Bless even the tiniest efforts and grow them into mira-

cles of faith and action and results! Amen and Amen!
In Jesus name, amen!

Tenacious-come-drag-us-back love

Dear Dad,
What drives me to this computer each morning to
pen words to you! I'm tired! It's nearly 4:00 am and
I've been up for an hour or two already! Maybe I
should just go back to bed.

Let me try praising and thanking you that usually
gets me going! What words shall I use? Will they ring
hollow in your ears? Will they echo with emptiness
throughout the halls of my soul?

You are a great God! A God infinitely wise and
more loving than myself! A God tougher and more tenacious in your efforts to rescue and to save than I can
imagine!

You are Linda (my wife) tough! Linda tenacious and
more! What love she loves me with! How much greater
is your love!

We give you thanks and praise for your love, for
your tenacious-come-drag-us-back love! I stray so often! Day by day, I forget the grace and love that calls
me! I substitute things for it of little value. I watch TV
when I could be in meditation and prayer and sweet
communion with you! And I do worse things than that!

Forgive me again and again, good Father! Restore
my feet to the path of righteousness!

I dream dreams and see visions, but rarely do I take
steps toward their fulfillment! I am so easily side-
tracked and dismayed!

Mold me shape me! Teach me the lessons time and time again and help me to apply them in daily living!

Some days I dread going to babysit but one smile from Maddie, one snuggle or hug from Karlie makes my day!

I love you, Father God! Brother Jesus with what love and determination and tenacity and audacity do you come to rescue, to transform, to save.

Dwell in us and round about us by your good Spirit. Do the messy work of making us new in you! The messy work of entering our messy lives!

I pray for our government and the governments of countries around the world! Raise up wise and godly leaders! Leaders who love their people! Leaders who love mercy and justice!

I pray for my friends! Make me slow to speak and quick to listen, bold to love!

I love you, Father God! Forgive us and renew us and make us one in you!

Amen and Amen! In Jesus Name, amen!

You are no small God!

Dear Dad,

Fresh are your mercies. Before the dawn, as we sleep, they refresh us! Each day is a new start in you!

You are great! You are wonderful and marvelous! Awesome in majesty and in all your works and ways! You are no small God! You created us and all things! By the word of your mouth, you spoke them into being! Through your good Spirit, you gave and sustain light and life!

When we rebelled and turned away from you, you sought us out! You called us back and gave your very life as a ransom for us!

None is like you! Awesome in majesty and power, yet humble and caring, tender hearted, loving, and merciful in all your ways!

Dwell in us and round about us! Let us live and move and have our being in you! Let our words and our actions be pleasing in your sight! Let your good and gracious kingdom come! Let the reign of evil and sin cease!

Let all the people praise you for your great salvation! Let your will be done in us and among us, even as it is in heaven!

Hear us for your name's sake! Look with mercy and forgiveness upon us! Recreate living and right hearts and minds within us and fill us to overflowing with your good Spirit! Give us peace and joy in our journey home to you and walk with us all the way! Let us celebrate with joy and laughter and grateful hearts at the lamb's high feast of victory and let us dwell in the house of our God and Father forever!

Amen and Amen! Walk with us this day and help us to discern and follow your lead! In Jesus Name, Amen!

I surrender unconditionally to your love

Dear Dad,

You are my light and my life! You are the one in whom I hope and trust! I have nothing to bring to you that you have not provided! I surrender unconditionally to your love and mercy and wisdom. I am broken and contrite, yet pride and sin of all sorts crouch waiting to overtake me!

You are God alone! You are my righteousness and joy! My courage and strength and ambition. I put my trust in you by the power of your good Spirit!

I rattle off many words to remind myself of your great mercy and love, of your forgiveness and generosity and glory! Thank you for your many blessings! Thank you for taking me through the hard times! Thank you for blessings and joys I do not deserve!

Increase love and wisdom! Increase plan and purpose! Increase generosity and goodness and peace and joy and love, with all good things!

How shall I thank and praise you for your great goodness and love! My mind boggles when I think of you! Your love is an enduring life-giving love!

Father God, I have dug myself into a deep hole especially as regards to my physical health. Let my dependence be on you! You are the one who forgives all our sins! You are the one who heals all our diseases! Let our hope and trust be in you! You lift up out of the pit! You make new and holy and one! Thy kingdom come! Thy will be done!

Turn us around, oh Father and Son and help us depend solely on you for our life and vitality and strength!

In Jesus Name! Amen!

I am good enough, even perfect

Dear Dad,

I give you thanks and praise for so many things! Things too numerous to list! Most especially, I thank you for your salvation in Christ and for the peace of knowing I am your child through Him!

Protect me as doubts try to creep in! Let me know that I am good enough, even perfect because of His all-availing sacrifice and love!

In that name, I pray! Amen and Amen!

You love with intention and reckless abandon!

Father God,

Here I am! Mold me shape me! Use me! Teach me! I am near the end of my rope. It will take a miracle to turn it all around, but you are the God of miracles!

You are our wisdom and our strength! You are the only one who has our best interest at heart! You love with intention and reckless abandon! You go through anything and everything to see us safely home with you!

Turn our hearts toward home! Let us seek you and find you, even as you have already found us! Let us bring other brothers and sisters along in the journey!

You are the one true God! You are the source of goodness and light and energy and love! You call into being! You set in motion! You sustain light and life! You make new and holy and whole and one!

You bless our efforts and good motives! You purify our desires! You give unique plan and purpose to our existence! You use and bless and multiply even our smallest efforts!

You are a bountiful and abundant God! A merciful and loving and patient God! You are light and life and goodness and mercy and generosity and strength.

Help me to walk with you this day. Help me to not give in to sin. Help me to do the things I am able to do. Help me to share your love with others! Draw me unto you! Help me celebrate and share the victory that is ours in your beloved Son, the Christ from eternity!

Teach me to discern open doors and to walk through them, asking for your blessing and going in your strength and power.

In Jesus name! Amen and Amen!

Life is messy sometimes!

Dear Dad,

Fell asleep early in the chair. Woke up about 10:40 and couldn't get back to sleep. The anxiety and depression were bad! I'm feeling a little less stressed now.

Oh Father, make me childlike in my trust of you! Make me totally dependent on you for all my needs! Let me live an authentic life in you! Let you be the one I run to! The one I turn to with my joys and sorrows with my cares and fears!

I spent several minutes crying! Crying for the people in the path of Hurricane Erma, the people of Puerto Rico! Crying for myself! Crying that we live in such abundance while so many do without! Crying tears of frustration because I can't or won't or don't know how to help myself and others!

I need your help and guidance and courage to get back on track or perhaps to take a new track, a better track! Still my mind and fears and help me to move forward one step at a time. It's 1:30 am, not sure whether to work a while or try to sleep.

Life is messy sometimes. Sometimes it's the mess that comes with laughter and joy and fun and friends! Sometimes it's the mess of trouble and hardship, of heartbreak and bad decisions! Sometimes it's the mess of doing the best you can in difficult situations or of choosing between multiple seemingly good options! Life is messy sometimes!

Hear us! Heal us! Let us claim and lay hold of all the riches won for us in Christ's death and resurrection! Let us live humble, courageous, authentic, generous, lives in Him!

I'm still weary, Father, and tears are spilling over again! Make them tears that cleanse and heal! Turn my crying into joy! Let my trust and my hope, my courage and my actions be in you! Still my anxious and fearful soul and set my eyes on you!

Amen and Amen and Amen! In Jesu Name

How do I go about listening for your voice

Dear Dad,

How do I go about listening for your voice? How do I go about hearing what you are saying to me? You are a great God and Father! You listen to me as I type my prayers and praises and my rants and raves! It occurred to me in Bible class yesterday that I am not a very good listener, at least when it comes to listening to you.

I met a man named Gerald yesterday. He was walking carrying a bedroll and stopped by a McDonalds. I stopped and asked him if he had had breakfast yet. He hadn't, so I bought him breakfast and we talked and ate for a few minutes. Then I gave him about 30 bucks wished him well and left.

I hope I helped him. I hope I didn't just contribute to his bad habits, cigarettes or alcohol or drugs. Father, look out after Gerald and all the homeless and bless our humble, even weak efforts to help.

Teach me Father, teach me to listen to you and to others. To ask questions without hidden agendas, not looking for openings to speak, but to truly listen to what others have to say!

Father God, I'm rambling again. I suspect, I need you to listen to me and I want to listen to you as well. Sometimes, I imagine what you might say to me or at least what I want to hear. I'm going to spend some time in silence now. Feel free to invade it with your voice or whatever you chose to bring to mind. I Love You Dad! In Jesus Name, Amen!

You parent us in perfect love

Father God, you are a great God! Kind and loving, merciful, and just and forgiving! You are always with us! Help us to trust you, to listen for your voice and to gladly follow! You are light and life! You are peace and joy and wellbeing! You are shalom!

We love you, though sometimes our thoughts and actions don't show it! We are grateful for your love and mercy and tender affection!

You parent us in perfect love, sometime tough sometimes tender! You delight in us! Teach us to delight in you!

Be our hearts desire and delight! Open us up to receive your love and presence and to share it abundantly with others!

Go with us now and bless and keep us and make us blessings one to another! Amen and Amen!

All this and more I dream of

Dear Dad, Father God,

Let my trust be in you! Let me find my hope and my joy, my strength, my courage, my wealth, and my very life in You! Keep my feet from evil and lead me in the paths you would have me to walk!

Teach me your ways, oh God! Teach them to me time and time again until I walk in them without stumbling! Teach me your ways and let my works be your works! Let me delight in your works and your ways! Let me find my joy in serving you and others! Prosper me in all things helpful! Grow within us and all about us fruit that endures to eternity!

Teach me your ways, oh God! And let me delight in the works of your hands! The seas are yours you made them! You called the dry lands into being! You set stars and planets, moons and suns, in their place! You called into being all living things! You shaped us in your own image! You breathed into us the breath of life and by your good spirit you made us living beings!

You pronounced it all good and then man sinned and messed it all up! Sin led to more sin, yet you were not content to let us perish in our sins! Through your seed, through your offspring, you brought salvation and hope! You completed what was lacking and set in motion the restoration of all things!

Your Son Jesus, Yeshua of old, the living word come down from heaven, took human form and lived as we could not live and died our death that we might live! He did not count equality with God as something to be grasped but humbly and courageously followed the path laid out for Him! Grant us His humility, grant us His courage and vision and hope! Let us follow where He leads and let us carry the crosses appointed for us!

Many have followed in his steps! Many have laid down their lives that we might live! Let us not shy away from whatever you are asking us to do! Let us boldly proclaim the goodness and salvation of our God!

We know not what lies before us whether easy things or hard, but we know, You are with us! Father, my will would be to regain my strength to be renewed as a youth of twenty or thirty, to live out my days with the wife of my youth, to see grandchildren and great grandchildren and great great-grandchildren! And dare I say it great-great-great-grandchildren or more! I would dwell in happiness and joy with my family around me! I would see 120 + years and be carried home to you as Elijah! All this and more I dream of! All this and more I imagine! Yet not my will but thine be done!

Give wisdom and love and courage and forgiveness in full measure, along with abundant and abounding hope and joy and peace! Let us bear with faithfulness and trust and joy and peace any hardships that come our way! Increase our faith, increase our hope and joy! Teach us to sow good seed into this world with an eye to an eternal harvest! Send us as laborers in your harvest!

Let the hope of all people be in you! Let all the people praise you! Prosper the works of our hands, the thoughts of our hearts and the words of our mouths! Let us bless and be blessed, even as you have showered us with blessings and gifts too numerous to count! Give us grateful and generous hearts!

Father, you know that we have not always managed money wisely! Time and time again we have borrowed from you, from your servants and from the poor! We are unable to pay back what we owe! You know that we have accumulated a mountain of debt that seems insurmountable! But with you nothing is impossible! Pay off our debts and restore to us your fortunes we have often squandered! Make us faithful stewards of not only your financial wealth but more importantly of the eternal treasures you have but in our hands!

Let love and joy and forgiveness and peace and healing flow from our hands into the lives of others! Let us loose the chains of poverty, homelessness, and despair! Continue to bless us and to make us blessings to many!

Make us the people you would have us to be so that whether we have this world's goods or not we may trust in you!

In Jesus Name, Amen!

Teach us, over and over and over again

Dear Dad,
Thanks for a new year with you! Thy kingdom come! Thy will be done!

Love us and lead us! Empower and equip us and call us to battle evil with your love! In big ways and in little! Teach us your ways, oh God! Teach us your ways!

Instruct us day by day! Teach us, over and over and over again, until we get it! Thy kingdom come! Thy will be done! In us and through us and to us and round about us! Thy kingdom come! Thy will be done!

Fan into flame the spark of goodness, light, and love that you have put within us! Burn brightly Spirit flame! Light our way! Warm our hearts and the lives of those around us!

You are a great God! Worthy of honor, love, obedience, and praise! Yet too often our hearts are just not in it! We type the words not so much in an effort to bring you thanks and praise, but to remind ourselves what a great God we serve! Thy Kingdom come! Thy will be done!

Love Us! Lead us! Transform us from the inside out! Make us new beings of light and love in you! There is stuff that needs doing and I don't know where to begin or how to proceed! Lead us! Guide us! Cause us to follow! Amen and Amen! In Jesus Name Amen!

Pep me up

Father God,

You are my strength and my joy! My hope and my salvation! In you do I trust! Let me not be discouraged or dismayed!

I fall so easily into worry and discouragement and apathy and laziness. Rescue me from all those things and more!

God of God and light of light and laughter and love! Increase in me the joy of my salvation! Restore to me my joy and hope, day by day!

You are light and life and love! In you do, I hope! In you will I trust! Thy kingdom come! Thy will be done! Love us! Lead us!

Pep me up, Father God! Encourage and uplift me! Restore hope and joy and godly ambition! Let me go in your strength and courage! Let me go in your hope and joy and peace! Thy kingdom come! Thy will be done! Love us! Lead us! In Jesus Name!

I wonder sometimes, why you put up with me!

Father God,

I wonder sometimes, why you put up with me! Why Linda puts up with me! Thank you and thank you for Linda! Not sure I know how I would have made it through life without her!

You are a great God and Father! A faithful friend and brother and savior! My counselor and coach! My advocate and my righteousness!

You give life! You give hope! You give plan and purpose to our being! Thy kingdom come! Thy will be done!

Bless this day! Bless our comings and our goings! Keep us mindful that our days are in your keeping! Give us grace and kick us in the pants when we need it! Thy kingdom come! Thy will be done! Love us! Lead us!

Delight in us and cause us to delight in you and one another! I pray for all my friends and acquaintances!

Draw us unto yourself! Make us holy and whole and one in you! Teach us to number our days aright! To give you thanks and praise to you for your great goodness and mercy! Teach us to incline our hearts and minds to wisdom and mercy and justice and love! Make us peace makers and reconcilers! Thy kingdom come! Thy will be done! Love us! Lead us!

Remind us that you are in charge! That you have the best interest of all people at heart! I pray for our president and other leaders and honestly, I don't know what to pray for them! I pray for the upcoming elections. Help me to discern how to vote or if to vote! Thy kingdom come! Thy will be done!

Going to close for this morning! Keep us this day and help us minister one to another! Amen and Amen! In Jesus Name, Amen!

Help me to love beyond the rah-rah

Dear Dad,
Draw me, draw me unto you! Draw me unto you and be my heart's delight and desire! Let me know your unsearchable love! Let me dwell in it and revel in it! Let it permeate my being! Let me love others with the love which with you love me! Make us one! Forgive us and lead us! Teach us to love tenderly and to exhibit tough love when needed! Thy kingdom come! Thy will be done!

Help me to love beyond the rah-rah, to love deeply and rightly! To hate sin and evil and to rejoice in goodness and beauty, love and light! Thy kingdom come! Thy will be done!

You are the great God! The only source of being and love and light and goodness and strength! Enlighten our ways! Strengthen and lengthen our days if it is helpful to us and others! Let us depend on you for wisdom and love and mercy and strength! Thy kingdom come! Thy will be done!

Praying now for my nephew. He called yesterday and we had a good visit. Watch over him and bless and keep him! Give him courage and wisdom and insight!

Teach all of us to love aright! Teach us to be generous and wise and loving and merciful! Help us with physical and mental and spiritual health! Let our hope and trust be in you!

Help me to breakthrough and give up my dependency on sin! Thy kingdom come! Thy will be done!

In Jesus Name, Amen!

I get carried away

Dear Dad, Father God, fount and source of all goodness and being and light and life,

What energy you give to your people, to your beings of light and love! (Not sure what prompted those last statements because I'm dragging a little this morning!)

Your word is living truth, living proof of your love for us! Fill us to overflowing with your love and truth! Bless us and make us blessings! Take us and make us into your living vessels of light and love! Let life giving rivers flow from our hearts and minds! From our very being, which is in you!

Keep us this day and every day! I turned 60 today, hard to imagine! At 46 I was so depressed that I never thought I would live to see 50, but you rescued me from the pit! You enlightened and enlivened me! You renewed my strength and my outlook on life!

What plans do you have in store for me, Father God! Even as I age, I dream of doing things that I'm not sure I have the energy to accomplish. Direct my path! Open my heart and mind and spirit to see your vision and your plan for me!

Father at 55 I dreamed of living 111 years and being carried away by you, now I dare to dream of living to 120 accompanied by my beautiful and faithful wife! Yet, my days are in your keeping! You know what is best for me and for all people! You have set eternity before us, so who are we to quibble about a few days on this planet! Thy will be done! Thy kingdom come!

Lead us and guide us all the days of our journey back to you, run to meet us and walk with us! Lead us and guide us for the way is treacherous and full of danger and trouble!

Let us not lose heart! Let us fix our eyes on you and on Jesus, the author and perfecter of our faith! Let us walk and not be weary! Let us run and not faint! Lift us up as on eagles' wings to fly!

Father, we would do great things for you! Yet it is not us, but your power at work within us that allows us to accomplish both humble things and great. We know not what lies before us! Let our trust and hope and joy be in you! Lead us and love us and carry us home in your arms!

Strengthen and encourage us for the days ahead! Whether they be many or few, for they are in your keeping and in you there is eternal life! In you there is eternal hope and joy and love! Bless us and keep us this day and always, for without you we perish! In you there is light and life and being! Let us live and move and have our being in you and in the Son and in the Spirit of life!

Call back the sons of men and the angels of light! Cause us to repent and return to you in tears and in joy! Forgive us and renew us! Let us find our names written in the lamb's book of life! You are God alone, and you delight in making us your own, true children! You transplant our sinful DNA with that of your Son! You mold us and reshape us once again in your image! You make us new! You make us one! One with you and one with all our brothers and sisters! You make us light of your Light and being of your being! (I get carried away when I contemplate your being and love, whether it is in your Spirit or just my own wild-eyed imaginings, I do not know!)

We give you thanks and praise for 60 undeserved years on this planet and we are bold to ask for 60 more! We are bold to ask that the ending of our days be even more glorious than the beginning! We ask for your grace and your strength! For your courage and your wisdom and love to finish strong in you! Yet not our will, but thine be done!

For your strength is made perfect in weakness, and by the grace of your outstretched hand we are sustained! You are our God and Father, make us like you! Give us grateful and wise and generous hearts to serve you and to love others all our days!

Let us bring an offering of thanksgiving and praise! Let us raise an opus of love and a chorus of praise to our God and Father! Let all the people love you! Let all the people praise you with acts of kindness and love! Change hearts and transform lives! Let all the people love one another and offer a chorus of joy and thanks and praise to our God! Let all the people praise You!

Give me energy plan and purpose, courage, wisdom, and love that I might live this day well! Let my trust, and my hope and my joy be in you! Let me live and move and find my being in you and in loving others!

God of God and light of life, how can I ever begin to thank you for grace upon grace! Father God, brother Jesus, life giving spirit, thank you! Thank you for your indwelling all-encompassing presence! Make us one! Love us and lead us!

Amen and Amen! In Jesus name Amen!

We do not comprehend it all

Dear Dad,

You are a great God! King of Kings and Lord of Lords! Creator and sustainer of all things! In you is hope and love and joy and peace! In you we find rest for our weary souls!

Oh Jesus, good Son, faithful brother, and friend, you are the way the truth and the life! You open yourself as the path back to the Father. You give yourself as food that sustains us and gives us new life in you and in the Father! Love us, lead us, good shepherd of the sheep! Guard and protect and encourage us, oh Lion of Judah! Feed us and nourish us, oh lamb of God!

You are light and life and love! You walked in our way and showed us a new and eternal way of living! You conquered death that we need no longer fear it! You are light and life and goodness, one with the Father! By your good Spirit, you include us in that one-ness!

We do not comprehend it all, but we know that if we love one another, you make your dwelling with us! You clean out all that is evil! You bind up and heal every broken part! Love us, lead us, transform us and make us new!

You are God of God and light of light, Very God of Very god! You are spirit and energy and light! You took our form for our sake! You created and recreated us in your image, in your very likeness! You make us true children of the Father! You transplant your DNA into us and transform ours until it is one with you!

Such ramblings and imaginings, such crazy words! You have adopted us as your children and by your good Spirit within us, you transform us unto your own!

Love us, lead us, oh Father of light and love! In-dwell us and overflow us that we may share you with a world deeply in need of you and your transforming love and Spirit! Breathe into us, oh breath of life, your love, and your truth!

You are the potter! We are the clay! Shape us into living vessels to transport your love to others, to pour into their lives the living water of your grace and love and mercy and forgiveness and hope and joy and peace! Water, that the Spirit can use to create new lives, washed clean from the inside out!

Living way, living word of life and hope, transform us and make us one in you! Love us! Lead us! Mold us! Make us! Empower and send us in your saving name proclaiming, "Yahweh saves!"

Repent and return to God, your Father! Walk in his ways and drink of his love and kindness, now and even unto eternity!

Multiply our humble gifts! We give ourselves to you! We offer ourselves as living sacrifices, praying use us, send us, transform us, and bless us! Multiply our humble efforts and acts of kindness and love that they may produce a rich and abundant and eternal harvest, an exorbitant return of righteousness, goodness, love, and souls!

Make us reconcilers and ambassadors of your love and mercy and grace! Give us your power and your authority and give us wisdom and love and mercy to use them for your good purpose!

Come, Holy Spirit, come! Come into us and transform us! Go out from us and save many souls! Use us and our efforts! Multiply and bless us and make us one!

Light of light and life, Holy Father, with the Son and the Spirit, Yahweh, great I am of all that exists! Let us not get too carried away by our thoughts, imaginings, and words! Let us not be so overcome by the revelations of your love that we forget to love each other! That we forget to love our neighbor and our enemy as ourselves!

Giver of all good gifts, provide this day for all our needs of body and soul and give us generous hearts to share your abundant gifts with others!

I pray for friends and family, all people! I pray especially for the homeless and the oppressed! Be their dwelling place, their comfort, and their hope!

Lead us in the paths that you would have us to go! Multiply and bless us in this journey home to you, that we may be received into your grace with many fellow travelers!

Amen and Amen in Jesus Name Amen!

Are they but ramblings of a mad man!

Dear Dad,

Dragging a little this morning again.

You are the great God and Father who listens to our fussing and our cussing! Who blesses us and moves us to action, in spite of it! You forgive our sins and short-comings! Help us to make it a good day today! Thy Kingdom come! Thy will be done! Love us and lead us!

You are light and life! You bring laughter and love and peace and joy to our existence! Love us! Lead us! Let our hope and our trust be in you! Be thou our cour-age and our wisdom and our strength from day to day! Thy Kingdom come! Thy will be done!

Shine on us and in us and light our way! Be thou our way and truth and life! Thy kingdom come! Thy will be done!

God of God, Son of man, mold us into your perfect and unique image! Make us like you! Teach us to love and forgive! Teach us to live in you! To abide in you and bear much fruit! Thy kingdom come! Thy will be done!

Giver of good gifts, You provide us with all we need! You are the one thing needful! In You we live and move and have our being! Apart from You, we can do no good thing! Make us whole in You! Make us one in You and with You!

Father, Son, and Holy Spirit, we name thee. Great Yahweh, I Am of old! I Am of our fathers! You are, therefore, we are! You came before all and are in all and by your good Spirit we have life! Truly in you and through you, do you live and move and find our being and our life! Such wonderings, such words to the describe you! Are they but ramblings of a mad man!

Teach us to love! Teach us to walk humbly and courageously with you and in you! Light our way! Be our way! For only in you is there light and life! Only in you is there plan and purpose, goodness, hope and joy! Thy kingdom come! Thy will be done!

Lead us oh living word! Lead us abiding Spirit of life and truth! Thy kingdom come! Thy will be done! In us and through us and round about us! In Jesus Name! For truly, Yahweh saves! Blessed be the name of Yahweh! Blessed be God! Amen!

You are the God who blesses and blesses!

Father God, dear abba Father, with Jesus the Son and Savior, by the power of the Spirit within us! Love us! Lead us!

Father, you are gracious! Loving and generous in all your ways! You want what's best for us and work for good in all things! Thy Kingdom come! Thy will be done!

You are the God who blesses and blesses! You are the God who shower's us with good things! You are the God who forgives all our sins and heals all our diseases! You are love and life incarnate! You dwell within us and give us new life in your Son, by the power of your good Spirit within us!

Father, feeling really grateful right now. Grateful for all the good things you have placed in our hands! Grateful for your patience with us! Beginning to dream a bit of all the good we could do with the Powerball jackpot. Thy Kingdom come! Thy will be done!

Not our will but thine be done! You know what is in our best interest and in the best interest of those around us! Mold us! Shape us lead us! Our days are in your keeping! In Jesus Name! Amen and Amen!

Perhaps I should just be still

Dear Dad,

Loving God and Father whose mercies and love are new every morning!

We thank you for keeping us this night and presenting us with the opportunities of a new day! Your love and your grace and your good Spirit uplift and sustain us! They make us new! They heal and restore our health and vitality! They make us one with you!

Teach us and lead us by the power of your good Spirit within us! You are light and life, love and truth and mercy and grace! Let us reflect these things to the world!

Light of light and God of God, Spirit being from whom all things gain their existence, incomprehensible person and energy and force and being! Lord of Lords, Very God of Very Gods, from eternity until life everlasting! We struggle to imagine it all! We probably get it all messed up as we ponder it, but we know that you love us! We believe that you are love itself, from which all things have their being, existence, and purpose! Indwell us and surround us and engulf us! Let us find ourselves in you, for apart from you we are nothing!

You build up and, in your wisdom, and perfect timing you tear down so that the new and perfect may rise in its place! Such ramblings and imaginings! Perhaps I should just be still in the presence of my God and absorb His essence and character, His wisdom and love and strength! For he has taught me what is good and what he requires, which is to act justly, love mercy, and walk humbly with Him.

God grant it in Jesus Name! Amen and Amen!

Shalom, what a word!

Dear Dad,
Shalom! You are my Shalom! My peace my wellness, my wholeness, and oneness and community of love and affection. In you I live and move! In you, I have my being and find shalom! Shalom is what I am seeking amidst this crazy world! I pray for shalom for all my friends and relatives!

Shalom what a word, peace and joy and health and wellness and harmony and wholeness and oneness and completeness and community and contentment and love and prosperity beyond understanding! Beyond seeming reality! All those things we have in you! All those things we possess in you! All those things are ours now even in the midst of a world full of their opposites!

Our Hello and our good-bye! The holding on and the letting go! The now and not yet! The near and the far! The sorrow and the joy! The kingdom of heaven! All are encompassed and indwelled in the shalom of God! Shalom, what a word!

Oh, prince of peace, shepherd of shalom, Father and Savior, brother, Spirit, and fiend, I am of all that exists! Grant us your shalom! Be thou our shalom! In Jesus Name! Yahweh saves! Blessed be the name of Yahweh! Shalom!

Father God, shalom is what I have been looking for, striving for and it is mine all along in you! Help me to live that out and to share it with a world desperately in need of shalom! Thy kingdom come Thy will be done! Shalom! And Amen!

Anxious to get started today!

Dear Dad,

I stall so easily throughout the day! Help me to keep moving forward and to pause occasionally and know that you are God! Thy kingdom come! Thy will be done!

Got the oil changed on the car yesterday! It cost about $ 20 or $ 30 dollars more than I was expecting, but the people who work there need your blessings as well. So, bless the money I spent there! Bless the people and their families and the people and families that they will spend that money on! Let it trickle down and be a blessing to many! Watch over our economy! Help us to remember that all good things come from you!

You are light and life and love! You are my anchor and my one constant in a fast-moving world! My rock and my fortress and my firm foundation! Bless me and what I build on that foundation! I commit all my ways to you! Let me not be ashamed! Keep my feet from falling and pick me up and set me on a firm path when I do!

Bless my friends! Bless the small group I am a part of! Thy kingdom come! Thy will be done! Love us! Lead us!

Anxious to get started today! Anxious to see what I can make of this day! Hopefully, I will surprise myself with some new-found energy, momentum and productivity! Thy kingdom come! Thy will be done! In Jesus name, amen and amen!

We live in the now and not yet of eternity

Dear Dad,

Your mercies are new every morning! I wake before the dawn to type out my thanks and praise to you! You are light and life and goodness and strength! In you is the fullness of joy! In you is light and life and purpose and being! You are with us when things are easy and good and you are with us when things get hard! You are the God of presence and peace! You shalom us with all good things! You work out even the hard times for good! You take the plans of the wicked and turn them to your good purpose! You work them out for the ultimate salvation and eternal good of many! Thy kingdom come! Thy will be done! Love us! Lead US!

Help me to remember all I do and am and write and say should glorify you and love and serve those around me! Thy kingdom come! Thy will be done! Love us! Lead us!

You are our source and sustenance, our creator, and our life! In you are all good things! In you is oneness and wellness and wholeness and wellbeing and life! Let us delight in you! Let us abide in you and bear much fruit! Thy kingdom come! Thy will be done!

Light of light and life and being and purpose, light our way! Be our way and truth and life! Our days and our purpose are in your keeping! Let us walk humbly and courageously with you as we truly love ourselves and others! Thy kingdom come! Thy will be done!

Grant peace and love, along with joy and all good things! Give us patience and perseverance and hope! Thy kingdom come! Thy will be done!

Still our fears and anxiety! Give us courage and strength, wisdom, and discernment! Make us steadfast in our trust of you! Make us steadfast in our commitment to love and serve you and others! Point us in the way we should go! Lead us by the hand, every step of this journey home!

We live in the now and not yet of eternity with you! We live in the foretaste of the joy and life to come! You have plans and purposes for us and all people beyond what we can think or dream or imagine! We pray humbly, send me! Equip me! Encourage me! And if not me, then someone else!

We commit our plans, our works and our ways unto you! We commit our bodies and minds, our feelings and emotions to you!

God of light and life, dwell in us and change us and make us new and whole and one in you! Thy kingdom come! Thy will be done!

Bless now this day! Bless our humble efforts to glorify you and to love one another! In Jesus Name! Amen and Amen!

Here I am! Such as I am!

Dear Dad,

Help me to always want to come and spend time with you! Thy Kingdom come! Thy will be done!

Oh Father God, here I am! Such as I am! Sometimes wanting to change for the better and sometimes not! Sometimes not willing to put in the work it will take to change! Thy kingdom come! Thy will be done! Love us! Lead us!

Open our ears to hear! Are hearts to listen and discern and follow and obey! Thy Kingdom come! Thy will be done! Love us! Lead Us!

We are weak and apt to falter and fall and fail! We are often hardhearted and unwilling to listen and follow! Open our hearts and minds to you! Transform us by the working of your good Spirit within us! Thy kingdom come! Thy will be done! Love us! Lead us!

You are light and life! You are our hope! You deliver and make new! You dwell within us and make us one and whole in you! You delight in us! Cause us to delight in you! Be thou our rock and our salvation! Our sure hope from day to day! Be thou our confidence and help! Our health and life and wellbeing! Be thou our one true treasure! Come to us and dwell with us and shalom us with your presence! Thy kingdom come! Thy will be done!

You are light and life! You are mercy and hope! You are our righteousness and our justifier! You are our advocate, our coach, and our friend! You are our all in all! Thank you for loving us! Thank you for caring for us! Thank you for blessing us with overflowing wealth and health and abundance! Thy kingdom come thy will be done!

Make us wise and loving generous and grateful. Love us! Lead us!

In Jesus Name! Amen and Amen!

He has redeemed us and paid the ransom price

Dear Dad,

Your Mercies are new every morning! I thank You, that day by day, I can come to you to thank and praise you and to pour out my heart to you!

You are God and Father, light and life and love! You come to me in the morning, and you refresh my soul throughout the day. You are always with me even at night you watch over me and keep me!

It's hard sometimes for me to feel your loving presence, but I know you are with me and that your good Spirit of life and love dwells in me! Keep me this day without sin, and if I fall, forgive me, and set me again on a right path!

Your works and your ways sometimes confound me, but I know that you love me! I know that to love and trust you and to love and act kindly to others is good and right!

Lead me in the paths you would have me to go. Lead me and love me and those around me! I pray for my family and friends and for all people everywhere!

Draw us unto yourself! Repent us and change our hearts and minds to love you and one another!

You are the God of the both-and! You laugh at our either or thinking! You delight in paradox and mystery! You excel in making your love and mercy evident in all you do! From the microbes that live in our gut to the stars and planets that fill the heavens, you have set things in their place with plan and purpose, that sin and evil cannot overcome!

When in our pride, we turned our faces away from you, you put in place protections for us! You waited eagerly for our return, and you sent your Son to seek us out and bring us back!

He is the way the truth and the life! No one returns to the Father but by him! He has opened the way back! He has sent us his good Spirit! He has redeemed us and paid the ransom price at the cost of his own life.

You, Yahweh, are God alone! You cause all things to be! You give them plan and purpose! Dwell in us and give us true life and oneness with you! Strengthen and encourage us minute by minute, for we are apt to wander and stray! Teach us to know the truth and to speak it with love to one another!

Thy word, Thy Son, is truth and life! The living word by whom you set all things in place! By whom you redeemed the whole world! Grant us his wisdom and his love and his peace, that with Him, we may pray, "Thy kingdom come! Thy will be done!"

Yes, that we may pray it and mean it and do it, by the power of your good spirit at work within us! Father, we have things to do today, seemingly menial things like cleaning the house and sorting mail, and yet you make the menial meaningful, magnificent, and even miraculous!

Open our eyes to see the things you would have us do! Put plan and meaning and purpose into our day! Let us spread your love and forgiveness and joy! Love us lead us! Thy will be done! Thy kingdom come!

Father we are bold to pray, heal us in body mind and spirit, pay off our debts, both material and eternal! We are bold to pray for miracles of healing for a friend! Let them rise up and walk! Increase our faith and theirs! We pray also, thy will be done, for we know that you can work through our infirmities as well as our strengths! But let that knowledge not be a copout to not believe you can and will heal!

Father as it is your will let miracles of healing break out in your church across the world! Let us cast out injustice and break every chain! Let us heal and make known your saving and transforming power! Thy kingdom come! Thy will be done!

Teach us to walk humbly and yet courageously with you all our days, whether they be long or short on this earth. Order our lives and our hearts and minds in love!

Amen and amen! In Jesus name we pray, for we are not ashamed to call him brother and savior and friend! In his name, yes! Yes! Amen!

You are the God who intervenes on our behalf

Dear Dad,

Continue to bless us and help us to discover new and better ways to be blessings to those around us! I pray for a friend having back surgery. I pray for comfort and healing and that she would know the joy and peace of your presence! Draw her, draw us, draw all people unto yourself! Change hearts and lives! Make us living vessels of justice and mercy and love! Change our lives and through us the lives of those around us! Thy kingdom come! Thy will be done!

I pray for friends and family members! Help me to reach out to them! Thy kingdom come! Thy will be done!

You are our God and Father! You are the source of all good things! You work all things out for goqd! Thy kingdom come! Thy will be done!

You are the God who intervenes on our behalf so that calamity and disaster never happens! You change events and history to protect us and to open doors of opportunity and blessing for us and those around us! You are a great God and Father! Loving and tender-hearted, full of lovingkindness and compassion and mercy and love! You parent us in the ways we need, each as you see fit! You are the God who knows and wants and cause the best things to happen to us and for us! Let our trust and our hope be in you! Thy kingdoms come! Thy will be done!

Give us grateful and generous hearts minds and spirits! Bless us and make us blessings to many! Thy kingdom come! Thy will be done!

You are light and life! In you do we live and have our being, because you dwell in us and around us! You are mighty to save! Let us abide in you and with you! Let the presence of your good Spirit make us a dwelling and a vessel fit for your service! Let the poor and needy find help and comfort and blessing through us! Make your righteousness shine as the noon day sun within us and through us! Let it spring forth as the dawn! Let it shine brightly all our days in this place! You are the God who sets us on a right path The God who calls us back saying repent and return to me! The God who indwells us so that we are even able to do those things! In repentance and in returning we are welcomed into your presence and find hope and purpose, joy and peace, and rest!

You are our shalom in this troubled land! You are our light in this dark place! You are our life in this valley of death and destruction! You are our spring in this desert and dry land! In you do we trust! You bring us good things! You bless us with joy and peace and prosperity and hope! You are our God and Father! Our savior and brother and friend! Our sustainer and our life from day to day! In you is life and hope and peace and rest! In you is the fullness of joy! Thy kingdom come! Thy will be done!

Father-God, blessed Abba-Father, Jesus, savior and brother and redeemer and friend, life giving spirit of truth and hope and love, we praise you and we bless you! Words cannot express our gratitude and our emotions! You shower us with mercy and loving kindness and too often we take it for granted! Too often we fail to extend the same love and kindness to others! Forgive us and renew us! Give plan and purpose and being to our existence! Thy kingdom come! Thy will be done!

Pay off our debts and fill us with such overflowing abundance that we cannot help but glorify you and share generously with others! You are the God of abundance and blessing! Help us to remember that we cannot out give you! Help us to remember that it is all yours anyway! Bless and multiply and use all you have placed in our care! House and home! Money! The cable TV! Our bills! You work these and all things out for good! Let us see with the eyes of faith! Give us true wisdom! Thy kingdom come! Thy will be done! In Jesus name amen and amen!

Bless now this day and all in it! Bless our comings and our goings! Guard our hearts and our minds, our words, and our actions! Amen and Amen! May it be so!

You scare me sometimes!

Dear Dad,

Up in the middle of the night and can't get back to sleep. Almost in a panic. Father God, I don't feel safe with you! You scare me sometimes! It's a love hate relationship! Forgive me for those words! I need to know you love me! I need to know I am safe with you!

You are my rock and my fortress in you will I trust and delight! I will have no fear, for you are on my side! You love me unconditionally! I am safe in your loving embrace! Safe in the big strong arms of my daddy-God!

Father, I do not want to make you into something you are not, but I need to know I am safe with you! "The thief comes to kill, steal and destroy, you come to give life and to give it to the full!" Together let's rid my life of false and hindering beliefs and fears! I am safe in you! I am loved by you! You want nothing but the best for me! In you will I hope and trust! Thy Kingdom come! Thy will be done on earth and in heaven!

"Have no fear little flock!" Be strong in me! Live in in me! Live and move and have your being in me! Thy kingdom come! Thy will be done!

You are safe and strong and perfect in me! I delight in you!

Love me lead me! Cast out fear and dread and despair! Cast out hatred and worry and anxiety! Live in newness of life! Live and laugh and love! Thy kingdom come! Thy will be done! Love us lead us. Father God!

You are light and love! You are forgiveness and reconciliation and hope and love! You fill us with all good things! You pour out an abundance on us! In you there is no scarcity or want! In you do we hope and trust! You are our rock and our shield! We let go of fear, and we rest and take refuge in you, oh Father God, oh source of love and life and being and strength!

As long as you give life and breath, we will put our hope and trust in you! You give life! You give plan and purpose and being and hope! Thy kingdom come! Thy will be done! Love us! Lead us! Help us to find our true being and purpose in you! Help us to live and move and have our being in you! Love us! Lead us! Thy kingdom come! Thy will be done!

Free us from the fear, dear Father and from every unhealthy belief that keeps us afraid! Thy kingdom come! Thy will be done! Love us! Lead us!

You are the God who loves us with a relentless and everlasting love! Father God, love us and lead us in your name and for your name's sake! In Jesus name! Amen and Amen!

Complete what is lacking in us!

Dear Dad,

Father God, thank you for hanging in there with me, for not giving up on me, even when at times I had almost given up on myself!

Father, I have not loved those around me as I should. Not sure why I am reluctant to call or contact people! Am I afraid of what they might think or how they might respond or of getting more entangled than I really want? Teach me to love as you would love! To care as you would care! Thy Kingdom come Thy will be done!

You are a great God and Father, deserving of faithful loving grateful obedient children and so often we have fallen short! Complete what is lacking in us! Love us into submission! Love us and care for us! I take you for granted! I am ungrateful! I shift the blame to others, even to you! Father, I try and try and fall short!

Forgive me! Renew me day by day, even as you already do!

Sustain my morning hope and joy and motivation! Sustain them throughout the day and even unto the evening! Give plan and purpose, mindfulness and meaning, intentionality and inspiration to my thoughts words and actions and being! Thy kingdom come! Thy will be done! Love us and lead us!

You are God and Father You are love and light and mercy and compassion! Love us! Lead us! Pay off our debts bless and multiply our meager gifts! Increase our love! Increase our compassion and generosity! Mold us shape us! Give us generous and grateful hearts that share with those in need! Thy kingdom come! Thy will be done! Love us! Lead us!

Delight in us and cause us to delight in you and in our brothers and sisters! Thy kingdom come! Thy will be done!

Make us like you! Make us loving and caring and compassionate and merciful! Thy kingdom come! Thy will be done!

In Jesus name! Amen!

I get so balled up with minutia!

Dear Dad,

I get so balled up with minutia! With the everyday stuff that doesn't really matter! Forgive me; restore my wandering feet! Let me use and share all your good gifts with gratitude and a generous heart! Thy kingdom come! Thy will be done! Love us! Lead us!

You are a great God! You are my rock and my fortress! My salvation and strong deliverer! You are my comforter and my strength! My courage from day to-day! In you, do I hope! In you, do I trust! Let me not be discouraged or dismayed! Thy kingdom come! Thy will be done! In you, will I persevere! In you, will I move forward!

Go with me this day! Keep me mindful of your love and care! Let me accomplish things that will move me forward in you! Thy kingdom come! Thy will be done! Love us! Lead us! Cause us to gladly follow! In Jesus Name! Amen and Amen!

Lead us home to ecstasy in you!

Dear Dad,

Another day passed and I am not really any closer to the things I want and dream about! It was not a bad day! We babysat the granddaughters. Bless those little ones and help us to minister to them, to lead and guide them in your ways! Help us to learn from them in their childlikeness! Thy Kingdom come! Thy will be done!

Saw the cardiologist, shopped, got car tags, paid the rent, napped stopped by a garage sale, ate out, went to the park, and topped everything off with ice cream, then baths! Pretty much ordinary, mundane stuff! You are the God, however, who blesses and multiplies and prospers and brings good things out of all things! You are the God who makes the ordinary, extraordinary! Who makes the mundane, miraculous! Bless all the small actions of the days past and of those to come! Bless and multiply and shape them into miracles of love and faith! Into redeemed souls and rewards and blessings beyond measure for us and many others! Thy kingdom come! Thy will be done!

Father God, I do not know if my days will be long or short in this place, for they are in your keeping! Help me to spend whatever time I have left wisely and to trust you and your amazing love for us!

Keep family and friends and bless and use and prosper them in your ways. Thy Kingdom come! Thy will be done!

You are a great God! Greatly to be thanked and praised! Let all the people praise you, oh God! From the greatest to the least! From the faithful, to the faithless, resurrect all your children and let them rise up to bring you offerings of unending thanks and praise! You are a great God, above all things! Above all and in all! You make new and good and right and holy! You redeem all things! Let all your children call you blessed! In you we live and move and have our being! In you do we exist and find being and plan and purpose! You love us and lead us and make us new and one in you! You delight in us and turn our hearts back to you and toward one another!

You are great! You are grand! You are good and glorious! You love us and have mercy on us and forgive us saying, "Return to the Lord, your God! Return to the Father and the Son by the power of the good Spirit within you!"

The wind of the spirit blows over us! You fill our lungs with life and purpose and being! Bless and prosper and multiply our days in this place. Bless our actions, and our being! Make us blessings to many, that they may glorify you! Thy kingdom come! Thy will be done!

Help us to love and live in you and in love and fellowship with one another! Bless now this day and all in it! Bless the thoughts of our minds, the words of our mouths, and the works of our hands! Do more with them than we can think or dream or begin to imagine! Blow our minds with your grace and love and blessings and lead us home to ecstasy in you! Amen and Amen! In Jesus Name Amen!

This could be a busy day!

Father God, this could be a busy day!

Run with me, Lord! Slow me down to a walk or cause me to stop and rest and appreciate things as needed. Or Lord, as it is your will let me fly and soar to new heights in you! Thy Kingdom Come! Thy will be done!

You are a great God and Father! You are the God who plans and ordains and brings to pass! Bless our day! Multiply our efforts and produce good and perfect and eternal results! Provide a rich harvest for our efforts and send many more workers into your harvest! Grant that we may plow and plant and harvest in proper seasons! That we may leave a bounty and abundance and stockpile and inheritance of good things for those who come after us! You are Lord of the harvest. Grant that, as it is your will, and if it is possible, that all might be saved and turn to you!

Oh God of mercy and grace, have mercy on us and all people! Forgive our sins and shortcomings and make us new and perfect and holy and one in your Son by the working of your precious and powerful Spirit! Make us as little children who love and depend on their abba Father, their daddy God!

Bless now this day and all in it! Give us what we need for this day and help and teach us to share generously from the abundance that is ours in you!

In Jesus name we pray! That name we proclaim saying, "YAHWEH saves!" Save us, Good Father of light and life, and make us one with you and your Son and all people! Amen!

Make us ambassadors of your love and grace!

Dear Dad,

Another good day, by my standards anyway. Thank You! Whether it was a good day, I'll leave to your discretion, but it certainly was a busy one and in my book, a productive one. Thank You!

Yes, thank you for some productive days! For relieving to some degree the pain in my knee and back! For helping me to get back on track and keep going! For allowing me to feel a little bit like my best self! Thy kingdom come! Thy will be done! Love us! Lead us!

Cause us to love ourselves aright and to love others as ourselves! Thy kingdom come! Thy will be done, in your perfect wisdom and timing and love!

Love us, lead us, and cause us to willingly follow you! You are a great God! Greatly to be thanked! Greatly to be praised! You have raised us up out of the pit of depression, anxiety, and despair! You have set us back on a firm path! Teach us to follow in the one true way that is you!

You are the way, the truth, and the life! In you we live and move and have our being! In you we find love and forgiveness, hope and joy! In you we find plan and purpose! Thy kingdom come! Thy will be done!

You provide for our needs, day by day! You provide and abundance that we may pay off our debts and share with others! You are a great God, loving, generous and faithful! You forgive all our sins and shortcomings and encourage and empower us to do better by the power of your good Spirit within us! You are faithful, Father, brother, savior, and friend! In you do the nations hope! To you do they turn when at last, they come to their senses! Let all the people praise you, oh God! Let all people and all nations bring you offerings of thanksgiving and praise!

You are our God and Father! You are the holy and righteous one, who was pierced for us, who laid down His life for us, and who took up that life again that we might have hope! That we might return to the Father and to our God! That we too might have life in you!

Abide with us and in us and cause us to abide in you and bear much fruit! Let your good Spirit transform us from the inside our and let rivers of love and justice and mercy and joy and peace overflow from our hearts and bless the lives of many! Thy kingdom come! Thy will be done!

Dwell in us and transform us and make us ambassadors of your love and grace! Amen and Amen! In Jesus Name Amen!

Surround us and sustain us in your shalom!

Dear Dad,
Tired and somewhat anxious today! Thy kingdom come! Thy will be done! Love us and lead us!

Father, not sure I'm into this, this morning, but I need to be! Give me your peace! Your shalom! A sense of wholeness and well-being in the midst of this crazy day ahead!

You are a great God! Shower me and fill me in and with your shalom! Restore to me peace and joy and a sense of well-being and adventure! Remove depression and anxiety and despair far from me! Thy kingdom come! Thy will be done!

Hold me and still me and move me to right action! You are a great God, full of love and mercy! You dwell in goodness and glory and shalom! Send us all those things! Grow them and increase them in our lives until we fully embrace them and the path you have set before us! God of gods and light of our being! You are the fullness of grace and love and mercy! Shalom us with your presence! Let your good Spirit warm us and comfort us and enlighten and empower us from the inside out! Surround us and sustain us in your shalom! Go with us this day! Forgive our sins and shortcomings and help us to do the same for those around us! Soothe and comfort us in our anxiety! Let us embrace you! Thy kingdom come! Thy will be done.!

Make us recipients of and participants in your shalom and set our minds always on you and others and how we may bring them into a relationship of shalom with you! Make us peacemakers, shalom specialists and strategists! Thy kingdom come! Thy will be done!

Go with us this day and keep us in your shalom that passes understanding! Amen and Amen! In Jesus Name! Amen!

Redeem the time!

Dear Dad,
Tired and a little bit worn out this morning. Yesterday wasn't the most productive of days from my perspective. I'm struggling to stay focused. Focused on you and on getting healthier and when I do it seems, I

let other things slide! Redeem the time! Reclaim it and bless it!

Father God, help us to formulate a plan, a plan to live generously and serve you and love those around us! Thy kingdom come! Thy will be done!

You are the great God and Father! You are our hope! You are the one who sustains our existence and causes us to survive and thrive! Thy kingdom come! Thy will be done!

Father, you know our heart and our mind and our motives! You know that we love you! Yet too often we have mixed emotions! Mixed loyalties! We do not always love you or those around us as we should! We do not often stop to think and even when we do, sometimes we make bad decisions, intentionally or unintentionally.

Forgive us! Renew us! Let us not be proud or wise in our own eyes, instead, give us your wisdom, your discernment! Your intentionality and intent! If we boast, let us not boast in ourselves, but in our great God!

You are light and life and love! You give plan and purpose and hope! You give joy and peace! Still our anxious hearts and minds! Let our trust be in you! Thy kingdom come! Thy will be done!

Give us grateful hearts! Hearts that are grateful for everyday things and hearts that are grateful for your salvation and mercy and grace! Thy kingdom come Thy will be done!

Bless a friend having surgery today, unless you have seen fit to miraculously heal her! Thy kingdom come! Thy will be done!

You are the God who knows what's best for us! Love us and lead us! In Jesus name! Amen and Amen!

Each day is a new start!

Dear Dad,

You forgive all my sins! Each day is a new start! Each day, I start fresh with you! You heal all my diseases! You lift me up out of the pit of depression and despair, destruction, and death! You shower me with good things! You renew my youthful vision and motivation, my vitality and strength! You are a great God! The only true God! You are greatly to be praised!

You are light and life and love! In you will I trust! In you will I hope! In you will I find courage and strength! Thy Kingdom come! Thy will be done! In Jesus Name Amen and Amen!

Your mercy in your Son exceeds them all!

Dear Dad,

You are the God who loves us and keeps us for your namesake and the sake of your Son! We do not always live up to your desires for us! Forgive us and change us! You are the God of power and might and justice, yet your mercy in your Son exceeds them all! Help us to not take that great love for granted! Help us to dwell in it and rejoice in it and to do all the good works you have prepared for us to do! Mold us! Shape us! Take away fear and doubt, along with indifference, laziness, greed and want and envy and pride, anger and unforgiveness and all such things! Replace them with all your good gifts! Thy Kingdom come! Thy will be done! In Jesus Name! Amen!

Don't let me take it for granted!

Dear Dad,
You are our God and Father! You build up! You make new! You are patient with us when we stumble and fall! You work for good in all things!

Father, I come here morning by morning to spend time with you and to remind myself of your great goodness, forgiveness, mercy, and love. And sometimes, I let the rest of the day get away from me! Help me to sustain my morning hope, vision, purpose, and energy! To carry out those dreams of things I will do! Help me to remember I am good enough as I am because of your love and acceptance, but don't let me take it for granted!

I come to you each morning confessing my sins and shortcomings; help me to do better! Help me to share your love and mercy and all things you have put in our care! Thy Kingdom come! Thy will be done!

Our days are in your keeping! I would have them be long and full of health and fruitful activity and service! (And sometimes I do little to make them that way!) Bolster my courage and intent and activity and energy! Heal all my diseases! Restore my health and vitality! Forgive my sins and help me to walk in your ways!

My days are in your keeping! You know what's best for me and all people! Go with us this day even as you have been with us all the days of this life! In Jesus name! Amen and Amen!

We know you love us and that is enough!

Dear God, You are a great God! The only true God and Father! Source of all that exists! We can't fully comprehend you, but we know you love us and that is enough!

Teach us, day by day, moment by moment to love others! To show mercy! Give us wisdom and discernment! Make us loving, merciful, generous and kind! Mold us, shape us into living vessels that carry your love and mercy to others! Thy Kingdom come! Thy will be done!

Teach us to walk humbly with you! Teach us to walk courageously with you! Teach us to care for the homeless, the hungry, the downtrodden and the oppressed! Thy Kingdom come! Thy will be done!

Make us wise and generous! Go with us this day, even as you have always gone with us! Keep us in your grace and mercy! Teach us to let go of every sin that entangles and snares us! To grow strong and healthy in mind, body, and spirit! Teach us to order our days aright and to incline our hearts and minds to wisdom and love!

Father, our days are in your keeping! Order them with what is best for us and others! Thy Kingdom come! Thy will be done! Love us and lead us and keep us, in Jesus Name! Amen!

You, oh Lord, are my righteousness!

Dear Dad,
I've been preoccupied with health stuff lately. Help me to remember that you are my health and my

strength! That You, number my days! And help me also to take good care of this body in which you dwell!

You, oh Lord, are my righteousness! I am covered in the robe of righteousness that your Son has provided for me! Be thou my joy and my courage and my life and breath, my hope and my song, my heart's delight! Let my trust be in you!

Father, we pray for all those between jobs. We pray for those sick and suffering in mind, body, and spirit; let your comfort and healing be upon them! We pray for those who do not know your love and mercy!

Love us! Lead Us! Give us joy and peace amidst the sadness of this earthy journey! Turn hearts and minds toward you! Cause them to repent and to come to you! We give you thanks and praise for your great goodness and mercy in our lives and pray that if it is possible it might extend to all people, everywhere! Thy kingdom come! Thy will be done! Love us and lead us in the paths you would have us walk!

Amen and Amen! In Jesus Name Amen!

Make us salt and light, in this rotting and dark world!

Dear Dad,

Waiting for the coffee to hopefully kick in. Been looking at the story of Joshua defending the Gibeonites and some of the surrounding verses. I have trouble making my knowledge of you gel with some of the things you supposedly asked your people to do and with the way they responded. You gave them a set of commandments about not killing and protecting our neighbor's home and property, then you send them in to totally destroy them. It doesn't fit and even if you did tell them, why didn't they talk back to you and politely refuse citing those very commandments you had given them? God of Gods and Lord of Lords, great I am who works all things out for good, You are that which you are and I can accept that! But you have taught me to love and I do not want to be a party to hatred or violence! Only in your Son, do we see the one not willing to fight back! The Yeshua of peace, of shalom who stands in contrast to those who have come before him!

So often we miss his message and example and invoke your name toward our hatred and violence! Forgive us good Father of life and love and hope! Forgive us for trying to make you into something you are not! Forgive us for not speaking up for our neighbor! Forgive us and lead us, great I am of body and soul, to be your beloved children! Have mercy on us and all people! Thy kingdom come thy will be done!

Make us salt and light, in this rotting and dark world! God of God, let us consider carefully, our words and our actions! How we will answer and what we will do! Thy kingdom come! Thy will be done!

Love us and lead us and cause us to pray for and to do your will! To advance your kingdom through goodness and light and mercy and justice! Thy kingdom come! Thy will be done! Love us! Lead us!

Let us not love this life more than we love you! Let us love you through loving our neighbor also! It is not an easy thing to turn away from hatred and violence! It is not an easy thing to not strike back! Have mercy on us and change our hearts and minds and being! Amen and Amen! In Jesus name! Amen!

Your righteousness and goodness fill the heavens!

Dear Dad,

Your Mercies are new every morning! Thank you! You are our God and Father! The Holy one! The creator and source and sustainer of all things! You set things in motion, and you maintain them! By the power and presence of your good Spirit you dwell in us and around us to uplift, encourage, empower, and sustain! By the word of your mouth, you call things into being! Thy kingdom come! Thy will be done! Love us! Lead us!

Your righteousness and goodness fill the heavens and it indwells us and makes us new and holy and one and whole in you! Love us lead us, even as you have done since before we were born!

Father God. your works and your ways are too marvelous for us! We can but catch a glimpse of your goodness and glory! You uplift! You sustain! You make new, day by day and in an instant! Time and space cannot contain you, yet you created them for your good purpose and our wellbeing! Your every thought is of love and justice and righteousness and goodness! You care for all you have made! Thy kingdom come! Thy will be done!

Forgive us our sins and shortcomings! Forgive us and renew us! Change our hearts and minds! Thy kingdom come! Thy will be done!

Light of light! I am that gives birth to all that exists! Primordial wisdom and being from eternity! The one who is and was and is to come! Fount and source of light and life! You sustain! You uphold! You uplift and encourage! Encourage and strengthen us in our way!

In Jesus Name, Amen!

It is all yours!

Dear Dad,

Pretty good day yesterday! Nothing spectacular. Just ordinary stuff for you to do miracles with!

Father, I want to get healthier! I want to get a handle on our finances! We want to love you and those around us! Give us servant hearts! Give us grateful hearts! Give us generous hearts!

Give wisdom and discernment and all good and helpful things in overflowing abundance and cause us to, joyfully and generously, share from the rich bounty you have put at our disposal! Keep us ever mindful that all we are and have and can do is but a trust from you! It is all yours! Make us faithful stewards! Make us joyful, willing, obedient children! Thy kingdom come Thy will be done!

Father, we ramble and write not for your sake but for ours! You know us and you know our needs and desires, but we don't always know ourselves as we should! We need your help and presence and guidance! We write to assure ourselves and remind ourselves of your great goodness and mercy! Bless us and keep us and send us and use us this day! Bless us and make us blessings one to another! Father God, we are all deformed children! We live with the terminal birth defect of sin! Sin we inherited! Yet your Son has overcome sin and death for us! Help us to live in that new life and hope! Help us to, gladly and generously, share it with those around us! How would you have me use and invest all that you have put in my care?

Father God, my days, whether long or short, are in your keeping! Help me to live each day as if life will never end and to live each day as if it were my last! In Jesus Name! Amen!

Help me to want to change!

Father, thank you for loving me! Thank you for forgiving me! Help me to love and forgive myself and others! Help me to want to change! In Jesus Name! Amen!

Make me like you!

Dear Dad,
Sorry! Or perhaps not! Not sure just what I'm feeling. Need to get going on a few things. A little out of kilter since this whole covid thing. Don't feel like doing much beyond maybe some straightening up. Don't feel much like writing, or any of a number of things I could be doing! Guess I'll try and get going on something and see where it leads.

Oh, Father God, dear Abba, my hope, and my trust are in you! Make me like you! Teach me your ways and help me walk in them! Give me a merciful, forgiving and loving heart, soul, and spirit! Make me generous and kind, loving and prosperous and productive. Give me diligence and determination and perseverance and self-discipline! Love me and lead me! In my weakness and laziness and fear give me your courage, ambition, and strength! Thy Kingdom come! Thy will be done! In Jesus name! Amen and Amen!

You are our light and our life!

Dear Dad,
Thank You! You are the great God and Father, the creator and redeemer, Savior, brother, and friend! You are the life-giving Spirit of goodness, love, and truth! You heal all our diseases! You Forgive all our sins! You renew our strength and vitality and hope! You lift us up out of the pit and rescue us from death, destruction, and despair! You are our light and our life! You are our heart's desire and delight, for you delight in us and shower us with tender loving kindness!

You, oh God, are our health and our strength! You are our source of healing and strength! Thy Kingdom Come! Thy will be done! Draw us unto yourself.! Bless us! Heal us! Lead us in your way, for you are the way, the truth. and the life! In Jesus name! Amen and Amen!

You restore our dreams!

Dear Dad,
You are the God, who heals all our diseases! You are the God, who forgives all our sins! You are the God, who builds up and encourages us! The God, who lifts us up out of the pit of death and destruction, of depression and despair! You renew our youth and vitality! You restore our dreams! You give wisdom and strength! Thy Kingdom come! Thy will be done!

You are our healer and our health! Let our hope and trust be in you!

In Jesus Name! Amen and Amen!

We cannot outgive you!

Father God, dear brother, Jesus, Holy Spirit, let my trust and my hope be in you! Draw me unto yourself! Dwell in me and change me! Mold me! Shape me! Use me for your good purpose! Love us and lead us!

Teach us to manage all you have put in our care wisely. Help us to return to you the first fruits, the best portion! Help us to use all your good gifts to help others, and to honor your name! Thy Kingdom come! Thy Will be done!

In my humanness and perhaps greed, I would like to win the lottery. I dream of all the people we could help. But, we have not always used money wisely! We have not always returned to you what is yours! Father it is all yours, we are but stewards and trustees! Help us to remember that we cannot outgive you! You are the God who showers us with good things, that we might help others! Thy Kingdom come! Thy will be done!

You know what is best or us! You give us your best gifts! Thy Kingdom come! Thy Will be done!

You, oh God, know how to bless and keep and parent your children with wisdom and with love! Bless and keep all your dear children! In Jesus Name! Amen!

You have said, "Yes!"

Dear Dad,

You have said, "Yes!" to so many things in my life! More yeses, than I can count! Yes, to family! Yes, to friends! Yes, to life! Yes, to extending my days! Yes, to better things than I asked for! Yes, to paying off our debts! Sometimes you have said, "No!" when it was not in my best interest, but always later you followed with an even better Yes! Sometimes, I suspect you said yes to things I insisted on in order that I might bear the consequences and learn from them! In so doing you said, "Yes!" to teaching me wisdom! You complete what is lacking in me! You said, "Yes!" to giving us eternal life in you and in your Son. Yes, to making us whole and one in you! Yes, to dwelling within us by your good Spirit! All your best gifts and promises are "yes" in your Son, who completed all things for us!

If I were going to write a new song to you, I'm not sure what the title would be. Just grateful for your love and forgiveness.! Thank you, dear Father for making me good enough, even perfect in Christ! Thank you that all our hopes and dreams and even more, are answered "Yes!" in Christ! Thy Kingdom come! Thy Will be done! In Jesus Name! Amen!

Help our love to not grow cold!

Dear Dad,

You, oh God, are generous beyond measure! You, oh God, have the eternal wellbeing of all people at heart!

You are Light and Life! You work for good in all things! You extend our days beyond what we deserve! You heal our diseases! You forgive our sins! You renew our youth and vitality and cause us to dream dreams and see visions of what could be! Thy Kingdom come! Thy will be done!

Father, the things of this world are fading away! Evil increases! Help our love to not grow cold! Fan it into flames and give wisdom, and discernment and knowledge! Give us wise and loving and generous hearts and minds! Faithful hearts and minds!

Teach us to trust you no matter what comes! Whether easy times or hard! Whether we win the lottery or not! Thy Kingdom come! Thy will be done!

Bless now this day and all in it!

In Jesus Name! Amen!

One more time and one more time

Dear Dad,

Here I am, Lord! Here I am, Father! I am, because you made me! You knit me together! You conceived my being, before time and space or perhaps not, I do not know! But I know that you love me! That you love and have compassion on all you have made! You are the God who proposes and brings forth good things! In you is light and life and love!

Had a fun day yesterday! Just ordinary stuff! Father, I appreciate all you give us and do for us but too often, I take it for granted and do not reciprocate in kind! Thy Kingdom come! Thy Will be done!

Forgive us! Renew us! Make us new and right and whole in you! Give us wise and generous hearts and minds! How often have I prayed those words! How often have I asked for chance after chance to change with seemingly so little progress!

Thank you, kind Father for being patient with me! Thank you, Jesus for saving me and completing all I cannot or will not do! So, Father one more time and one more time and one more time again as long as it takes, lay hold of me! Change me! Change us! Draw us unto yourself and unto each other! Give wisdom and courage and love! Make us wise and joyfully obedient! Give us humble, servant hearts! Let us trust in you not in the things you so generously provide! Thy Kingdom come! Thy Will be done! Love us! Lead us!

Transform us and make us new in you! Pay off our debts and let us share generously from the abundance of your love and mercy! Thy Kingdom come! Thy Will be done! Love us! Lead us!

Help us to see the way you would have us go! Thy kingdom come! Thy will be done!

You are light and life and love! Dwell in use to encourage and enliven and empower us!

In Jesus Name! Amen and Amen!

Often, I have wasted my gifts!

Dear Dad,

Slept well and long last night. Dreamed a couple of dreams about youth trips and being a DCE, but the events and people were all scrambled together! Mostly, they were happy dreams though! There is a temptation to stay in the land of our dreams and not to move into the sometimes harsh reality of the light, but into the new day we must go.

Father feeling a little like a failure this morning! Like I let you down! Let my family down! Let me down! Woke up thinking I was a mediocre DCE at best, but I guess perhaps I touched a few lives.

I've let my health go. A few weeks ago, I was all gung-ho to reclaim it but some of that ambition has waned the last few days or so. I slipped back into some old eating habits and I don't remember the last time I went to the Y or exercised intentionally at home!

I've slipped into sin and indifference in other areas of my life as well. Oh, Father God, I know that all things are possible with you! Help me to become in my old age the person I often sought unsuccessfully to be in my youth! Help me to use the talents and abilities I have left and renew at least some of my youthful vitality and strength! Father, if it is not too late lift me up and make me new and holy and one again in you! Thy Kingdom come! Thy will be done!

Father God, You are the keeper of our days! You determine their length and purpose! Often, I have wasted my gifts! Often, I have not lived my life to the full in you! Let not my sins both great and small keep me from loving and serving you! Uphold me with your right hand! Fill me with your good Spirit! Give energy and motivation and perseverance and strength and love and wisdom to my latter days! Renew me and lift me as on eagle's wings! Mold me shape me! Let my trust and my hope be in you! Protect us from sin and evil and sickness and death! Thy kingdom come! Thy will be done! Love us! Lead us!

Delight in us again and be thou the delight and desire of our heart and mind! Sustain and strengthen our morning hope throughout the day and give us refreshing rest each night! Cause us to do the things that build us up and that build up the people around us! Thy Kingdom come! Thy will be done!

You are light and life and goodness and mercy and wisdom and strength! You never give up on us! Help us to not give up on ourselves and those around us! You renew our strength! You give joy and peace and purpose to our latter days! You lift up! You make new! Help us, dear Father! Help us faithful brother and friend! Help us life-giving Spirit of shalom and power and grace! Sustain us and bless our sometimes too meager efforts! Teach us when to push on and when to rest in you! Be thou our strength and sustenance and life! Thy Kingdom come! Thy will be done! In Jesus Name! Amen and Amen!

Together let's make it a good day! A day that counts for eternity! Amen!

Teach us to walk away from sin!

Father God,

You are the great creator, healer, and sustainer! You forgive all our sins, for Jesus' sake! You love us with and everlasting love! You draw us unto yourself and unto your Son. You cause us to believe and trust in Him and in You, by the power of your good Spirit!

Teach us to walk away from sin! To forsake sinning and dwell in your mercy and strength! Mold us and shape us and use us! Let our delight be in you! Be thou the desire and delight of our heart and mind! Thy kingdom come! Thy will be done!

You forgive all our sins! You heal all our diseases! You lift us out of the pit of destruction.! You restore health and hope and joy and motivation and love! You make new! You make whole and one! You are our light and our life! You are always with us, even unto the end of the age! You are there in easy times and in hard times! Thy kingdom come! Thy will be done! Love us and lead us!

Help us to hear your voice! Help us to follow where you lead! Watch over us and protect us and guide us in Jesus name! Amen and Amen! Yahweh Saves! Blessed be the name of Yahweh!

In you we find plan and purpose for being!

Dear Dad,

You, oh Father, are the great healer of body and mind and soul! You lift up out of the pit of destruction! You renew our youth and vitality! You extend our days for mercy sake! You heal all our diseases! You forgive all our sins! You are light and life and love! In you we find plan and purpose for being! In you we live and move and have our being! You are beyond our comprehension! By your good Spirit, we walk humbly and courageously with you and demonstrate your love and mercy and justice to those around us! Thy will be done!

You are a great God and Father! You are the great healer of body and soul! You are the faithful Savior, redeemer, and friend! You are the life-giving spirit of love and life and truth! We thank and praise you for your great mercy and love! In Jesus name! Amen!

You are not afraid to share your glory

Dear Dad,

Help me to get back on track. Your works and your ways are marvelous in our sight and yet too often we forget about them and don't walk in them.

Teach me, mold me, shape me! Help me to keep all things in proper perspective. Help me to keep my life focused on you and on your Son.

You are God and Father. You are light and life and love! You lift up and exalt! You put the proud in their place! Help me to walk humbly yet courageously in you! To do your works and walk in your ways!

You are a great God, Lord of all and yet you don't lord it over us but are just and merciful, loving, and full of kindness! You are not afraid to share your glory; you created us in your image and recreated us in the image of your Son! You set your good Spirit within us saying be fruitful and multiply and produce much fruit in me!

Love us! Lead Us! Walk with us and dwell in us and round about us! Cause our hearts to repent! Cause us to walk in your paths!

Let us behold your face and live! Let our lives emanate your glory, even as Mose' face shone after being in your presence! Let us live and move and find our being and purpose in you!

God of God, Father God, Daddy God even Abba Father, shine in us and through us and round about us!

Thy kingdom come! Thy will be done! May your name be hallowed among us! Provide for our needs and wants, day by day and give us generous hearts to share from your rich and abundant bounty! Forgive us and teach us to forgive! Protect us from evil and temptation! Let us bring you offerings of thanksgiving and praise!

Indeed, let all the people praise you, oh God! Let all the people come to you in thanksgiving and praise! Amen and Amen!

In Jesus Name Amen!

Spur us on in love and hope

Dear Dad,

Thy works and thy ways are marvelous and sometimes confusing to us! We believe and do our best to trust that you are a loving God, full of kindness and compassion! That your heart's desire is for all to be saved! Love us and lead us and turn our hearts toward one another! Thy kingdom come! Thy will be done!

Help me to turn it around to make the changes I need to make! Thy Kingdom come Thy will be done!

Love us and lead us! Great God! I am of all that exists! Father and brother, Savior, friend, kind mother, spirit of life and truth and grace, the family of God, One in truth and grace! (And I don't have a clue what I'm rambling about!)

You are God! You are comforter and loving confronter! Confront us and comfort us and change us into your loving children of light and life! Thy kingdom come! Thy will be done in us and through us and round about us! Be thou our all in all, our hearts desire! Love us and lead us! Thy kingdom come! Thy will be done!

Lead us in the paths we should go! Lead us and love us and cause us to love others! Thy Kingdom come! Thy will be done!

Go with us this day and keep us and spur us on in love and hope and mercy and grace! Amen and Amen! In Jesus name Amen!

It is hard to turn to you when we sin

Dear Dad,

Not quite sure what to do with yesterday. It was a pretty fair day in many ways. The evening wasn't good though. Guess I was pouting maybe or something! Anyway, it didn't go well! I'm sorry but my apology seems hollow to me, because I know it will probably happen again! Forgive me and set me on a right path!

It is hard to turn to you when we sin, but you alone are the one to whom we must turn! The one in whom there is forgiveness and mercy and grace! The one in whom is newness of life and hope and purpose and joy! So, forgive us Father! Repent us and turn us from sin and evil and despair! Love us and lead us! Help us to walk in your ways! Thy kingdom come! Thy will be done!

Father sometimes too, we take you for granted when things are going well. We think we're doing it on our own. But all we are, our abilities and motivation come from you! Help us to remember that! Help us to always turn to you when we are doing well and when we mess up!

Bless this day! Bless us and all in it! Bless us and make us blessings one to another!

In Jesus Name, Amen!

Fill us with your great love and mercy!

Dear Dad,

Your mercies are new every morning! Fill us with your great love and mercy! Let it become a spring, welling up inside of us, bringing us life and wisdom and truth and love! May it spill over into the lives of others! Continue to bless us and to make us a blessing to others! Give us grateful and generous hearts and minds! Let our good intentions be translated into actions of love and mercy and kindness!

You are a God of life and light! You love all your children! You set them in their proper place! Teach us contentment! Teach us peace and joy! Teach us to walk in your ways! Love us! lead us!

Teach us to walk humbly and gratefully with you! Teach us to act with courage and kindness, wisdom and love! You are God of God, light of light and laughter and love! You build up and when you tear down, it is for our benefit that you may build better in its place! Love Us! Lead us!

You are God of God, light of light! You know how to bless all your children! You know how to love each of them best! Teach us not to be envious, but to accept all good things from your hand with gratitude and love for others in our hearts! Love Us! Lead Us! Bless us and care for us with your perfect care! When hard things come, use them to make us better not bitter!

You are God of God! Even very God of Very God! You are loving Father! Love us! Lead Us! Grant wisdom and joy and peace and love!

Amen and Amen! In Jesus Name, Amen!

Let us not go to the dark side of our being

Dear Dad

Tired this morning. Was dragging most of the day yesterday, weather, poor sleep, flue shot or some combination of the above! Not a very productive or rewarding or energizing day. There were some good spots though! Thy kingdom come! Thy will be done!

Not in to this this morning! You are a great God worthy of honor, love, thanksgiving, and praise! So often do we take your great love and mercy for granted How often do we forget the blessings and responsibilities and privileges that come with being your children. How often do we fail to love our brothers and sisters as ourselves! Thy kingdom come! Thy will be done!

Light fires under us and fan into flame your Spirit of goodness and love! Unite us! Ignite us! Empower and equip us and cause us to share your love with others, in little ways and in big ways! Thy kingdom come! Thy will be done! Love us and lead us!

Cause us to pray, "Thy kingdom come! Thy will be done!" Cause us to desire it and work for it and to receive it by the power of your good Spirit within us! Let us not go to the dark side of our being, but dwell in your light and your love! Thy kingdom Come! Thy will be Done! Love us and lead us!

Encourage and motivate us and cause us to act in your love! In Jesus Name and in the power and sufficiency of that name do we pray! Come, Lord Jesus, Come! Come Holy Spirit come! Mold us and shape us and use us!

Amen and Amen

Truly you are the God who redeems and saves!

Dear Dad,

You are the great God and Father! My creator and sustainer, who causes me to survive and thrive! In you do I hope! In you do I trust! Increase my faith!

You give wisdom! You are hope and joy! In you my soul delights! Thy kingdom come! Thy will be done!

You are light and life! In you is the fullness of joy and peace! In you, I live and move and have my being! In you, I find plan and purpose and being! You love us with a relentless, enduring, everlasting, love! You turn our hearts again to you! Your loving kindness and mercy inspires us to be like you! You give life! You give hope and joy, plan and purpose! You delight in us and in all you have made! It is our pleasure to thank and praise you and to love those around us! Thy Kingdom come! Thy Will be done! Love us! Lead us!

Make us your holy people, your true and beloved children! Thy kingdom come Thy will be done!

In Jesus Name! Amen and Amen! Truly you are the God who redeems and saves! Blessed be your name forever! Amen!

Feeling afraid and out of control!

Dear Dad

Feeling afraid and out of control! Really felt it last night! Not much of anything we planned came together yesterday The result, I think, was that I felt out of control, afraid and anxiety riddled.

Why isn't it easy, to just trust you! To place things out of our control into your hands! Forgive us, Father God! Love me! Lead me! Protect me!

Father God, I don't want to die! That's what a lot of this comes down to. It's a trust and will issue in many ways! Teach me to trust you, to pray thy kingdom come, thy will be done and to mean it! Teach me to know and believe and hold on to the truth that the things of this world cannot compare to the glories to be revealed to us! Thy kingdom come! Thy will be done! Love us and lead us, gracious Father of goodness and light!

Thank you! We praise you for your goodness and mercy and love! You get us through hard times! You are light and life and love! You are health and wealth and strength! You help us to persevere! You cause us to survive and thrive in a hard land! You fill us with good things, so that we cannot help but share from our abundance! Thy kingdom come! Thy will be done! Love us and lead us, gracious Father!

Into your hands we commit our lives and plans and purpose and being! Our days are in your keeping!

In Jesus Name, Amen and Amen!

You, oh Father, are a great God!

You, oh Father, are a great God! A great provider and teacher and friend! You are patient and forgiving, loving, merciful, and kind! Lead us in your ways and cause us to follow!

In Jesus Name! Amen and Amen!

Thank you for forgiving my sin!

Dear Dad,

Here I am again. Thank you for another day! Thank you for forgiving my sin! For being patient with me and my shortcomings and sin!

Mold me shape me! Help me! Cleanse me! Purify and protect me, in Jesus name. Amen!

Father, You are my health and my healer! You forgive all my sins! You heal all my diseases! You lengthen my days for mercy's sake and because I have asked! You shower me with good things! You lift me out of the pit of destruction and despair. You restore my hope and joy! You renew my vitality and strength!

You are a great God and Father! You are the creator and sustainer of all that exists! You number our days in mercy! You use and multiply our humble acts of service! Your good Spirit works within us to help us to walk humbly and courageously with you!

You are light and life and love! In you do we find our plan and purpose! In you do we have life and being! Walk with us this day also and make it productive and fruitful in your sight!

In you do we hope! Let our trust also be in you! In Jesus Name! Amen and Amen!

You are our great God and Father!

You are our great God and Father! You are the one who made us and gave us life and plan and purpose and being.

You give hope! You cause us to trust in you and in your Son by the power of your good Spirit at work within us! You are the light and life of the world! You build up and make new! You forgive all our sins and shortcomings! You heal all our diseases and rescue and redeem us from the pit of destruction and despair! You renew youth and vitality! You bless us with good things from your hand!

We love you because you first loved us! Your works and your ways, we often don't understand, yet we know you love us and want for what is best for us and all people! You work for good in all things! You love with eternal purpose in mind!

You bless and bless and make us a blessing! Go with us this day and help us to follow your lead!

In Jesus name! Amen and Amen!

You are the still point of our existence!

You, Oh God, make new and holy and one! You lift up! You heal all our diseases! You forgive all our sins! You are light of light, God of God, only true God, the creator and sustainer of all things! You set things in motion and keep them spinning. You are our rock! You are the still point of our existence! Help us to be still and know that you are God! In Jesus Name! Amen!

So very tired of holding it together!

Dear Dad,

Sitting here at 3:00 am anxious and crying. Still my soul. Calm my fears. Don't know exactly what spawned this attack of anxiety. Just got overwhelmed with things.

Tired, Father God! So very tired of holding it together! Met with my counselor yesterday and that went well. Thy kingdom come Thy will be done! Love us and lead us!

God of God, Lord of Lords, even daddy God of daddy God, strengthen me by thy good spirit! Return to me the joy of your salvation and presence! Walk with me! Run with me! Lead me and guide me! Celebrate with me! Thy kingdom come Thy will be done! Love us and lead us!

Enlighten and encourage and equip and empower us! We have things to do! We have things to let go of and things to hold on to! Help us to discern which are which! We need to regroup and attack things head on! We need to go on the offensive and share Your love and mercy and forgiveness with others! Thy kingdom come! Thy will be done!

You are a great God! You are mighty to save! You lift up the downtrodden and you still all our fears! Go with us and protect us! Motivate and sustain us by your good Spirit and by your living word! Build us up and train us in mind, body, and spirit! Thy kingdom come! Thy will be done!

Great is our God in the heavens and on the earth! He fills all the empty spaces with his presence! He creates and sustains and causes to thrive! He goes with us and supports us! He transforms us and uplifts us! None is like him! He is mighty to save! He dwells in light! Love, mercy, and justice are his handiwork! He rescues and saves! He draws near to us! He carries us home in his arms!

Sustain us and uplift us and cause us to thrive in you and with you! Be thou our path, our way, our guide and our God on this journey home! You welcome us and you celebrate with us, though we do not even deserve to be called your servant or slave!

Teach us your ways! Help us to extend love and kindness, goodness, and mercy to those around us! Give us wise and generous hearts! Make us know for certain, that we cannot out give God! Keep us mindful that all that we are and have and can do is a gift and trust from you! Give us humble and courageous hearts, minds, souls, hands, and voices! Help us to walk with you and serve you! Thy kingdom come! Thy will be done!

Love us and lead us, this day and all the days of our earthly existence! Thy kingdom come! Thy will be done, in us and through us and round about us! In Jesus Name, Amen and Amen! Yahweh saves! Amen!

Father sin is such an ugly word!

Dear Dad,
Blew it again last night and at least a part of me doesn't even wish to call it sin. Father sin is such an ug-

ly word! We prefer shortcomings or flaws or ... I don't know what! But sin creeps back into our lives.!

We have our pet sins like overeating, that we don't even want to call sin. They are the ways we cope with the stresses of life! The ways we gratify ourselves in the moment and divert ourselves from things we don't want to deal with. Things we get enjoyment from. Pleasurable things, but things that sometimes cause us trouble in the long run. Things like shopping and eating and watching TV.

Father God what do you expect from us bags of clay and water? Dear Jesus, how did you live the perfect life and avoid the sin we so easily give in to? We struggle so hard at times, and often, Father, our guilty consciences cause us to turn from you to try and run from you or hide from you!

We ascribe to you thoughts and emotions and actions that it is not be fair to ascribe to you! We take the worst in us and ascribe those things to you, when sometimes I think we are nothing like you! Rambling Father God, dear Abba Father!

I keep running back to you day by day! I run back to you because I can find forgiveness and love and mercy and understanding nowhere else!

Father God, I do not understand my behaviors at times! I do not understand why I do things that are not helpful, that are harmful, that are sin! Forgive us, good Father! Teach us to turn to you in the midst of our struggles, for indeed you are with us always!

Thank you, Father God, dear brother Jesus and life-giving Spirit for going with me to places you would rather not go! Places that are harmful to me or others!

Father God, we are prone to so many things, like anger! Like overeating! There is always stuff, Father! Stuff, that causes us to worry, to overeat, to get angry, to divert with TV, and other things! Father God, forgive us, but more importantly change us!

I don't like to think you punish us for our sins, but rather that we receive the consequences for them! The consequences are too great, eternal separation from you! We need you and your Son to spare us the consequences of sin!

Father God, my thinking gets so balled up! There is a force, an entity, a being in this world that causes all sorts of pain and suffering and violence and evil! A force that would have us call evil, good and good, evil! A force that would do away with sin and guilt! Yet at the same time, he/it is the accuser that piles on the guilt! The one that would blame God for all the sin and trouble, we cause ourselves and others! The one that would cause us to turn away from God, to question his motives and his actions, to believe that God wants to hurt us and that He does not have our best interest at heart!

Forgive us, good Father and set us back on a good path! Cause us to see and to seek and to do good things! Thy kingdom come! Thy will be done!

Father, forgive us for Jesus' sake! Cause us to dwell in you and to abide in you and your care! Turn us from things that are not helpful to us! Things that hurt us and those around us! Things that provide immediate pleasure, but no lasting joy or peace or purpose! Father God, we do not always know what is good or helpful, but we trust that you are the God, the one, the source, that works all things out for good! The one who sees with proper perspective! The one who has our best interest and the best interest of all people at heart!

Make us like you, loving and merciful and just and full of loving kindness, mercy, and compassion! Thy kingdom come! Thy will be done!

Father God, we have racked up debts we cannot pay ourselves! Financial debts, debts of poor health, debts of broken relationships and hurt feelings! Debts only you can repay! Maybe we need to suffer the consequences of our actions for our own eternal well-being or maybe with your help we can turn things around in the here and now!

Let our trust be in you! Let our hope and our joy be in you! You are the faithful God! You are the forgiving God! You are the loving and merciful God! You are our light, our life and salvation! Help us to remember that!

Father, our days are in your keeping! Help us to remember that! Help us to live each day as if it were our last on the one hand and as if we had an eternity to enjoy with you on the other! Let us not take your great love for granted! Thy kingdom come! Thy will be done!

Make us one in you and with you! Make us whole in you and with you! One and whole with you and with one another! In Jesus Name! Amen and Amen!

You fill our lives with an abundance of good things!

Dear Dad,
Yesterday was a struggle in many ways. Anxiety and overeating still plague me! Give me wisdom and

courage in all this! Remove anxiety and fear far from me, that I may push forward in you!

So much seems out of our control right now! Help us to exercise control in those things we can control and to commit into your hands those things which are beyond our control. Thy kingdom come! Thy will be done! Love us and lead us, gracious Father!

You are light and life and goodness and courage and wisdom and strength and mercy and love! You shalom us with your presence! You fill our lives with an abundance of good things! We give you thanks and praise for who you are and for all that you do!

You love us with an enduring, everlasting love! Help us to love as you do! Help us to recognize and accept and live in the wisdom and love you so generously shower upon us! Lead us in your truth and love and justice and mercy! Thy Kingdom come! Thy will be done!

In Jesus name! Amen And Amen!

To love is a good thing!

Dear Dad,

Watching Maddie today! She's pretty cute! Multitasking, eating, playing dolls, and watching the iPad all at the same time.

You are a great God! Loving Father, friend, savior, and brother and Lord! You are the life giving, transforming Spirit! Where would I be without you!

It is you who gives plan and purpose to our existence! You who directs our paths, for us and sometimes in spite of us! We do not always know what's best for ourselves, and so we commit our plans to you, trusting that you will work things out in our best interest! Love us! Lead us! Magnify and multiply the works of our hands to have lasting and eternal benefits for ourselves and others!

You are light and life and love, eternal energy, and source of all that exists! You hold it all together! You cause things to function with plan and purpose! You have created dimensions within dimensions, worlds and planes and things we cannot begin to understand or imagine! In humility we walk with you, for your ways are higher than the heavens and beyond our comprehension!

Still, we know that to love is a good thing! To act kindly, with mercy and compassion is godlike and good! Guide us and direct us in the things we do! Prosper us in all things helpful! Give plan and purpose and meaning to our earthly existence!

We give ourselves as living sacrifices! We offer thanksgiving and praise as our offering, for it is all we have to give! Everything we are and can do is a trust from you! Teach us to abide in you and bear much fruit! Teach us to invest our lives in things that last and produce an exorbitant return of righteousness, goodness, and souls!

God of God, source of all righteousness and good gifts, pay off our debts in your perfect timing and cause us to number and order our days on this earth aright! Whether they be long or short, they are in your keeping!

We have not always made wise decisions, but you oh God, turn even foolishness to wisdom and profit! Bless and multiply and provide an overflowing abundance of all things good and profitable for body and soul! We pray for friends and family in need of your presence and care! Love us, lead us! Thy Kingdom come! Thy will be done, in the hard things and in the easy, in the seemingly good and the seemingly bad of this life! Let all things work together to bring about your plan and good purpose for us and all people!

Let all the people praise you, oh God! Let all the people thank and praise you!

I'm on to other things, just what I do not know! Prosper and guide me!

In Jesus Name! Amen and Amen!

Father, we are plagued by so many things

Dear Dad,

Dragging a little this morning! Been kind of up and down lately. I thought I was in a better place! Help me to hold it together! To get my stuff together and not forget where I put it! Help me to live and survive and thrive in you and in your Son!

God of God, light of light and life and love, dwell in us and draw us unto yourself! You are God and Father! You are faithful Savior and brother and friend! Make us like you! Give joy and peace and all good and helpful things in abundance! Help us to receive them with grateful hearts and teach us to be generous! Let your love flow into us to transform us and flow out of us to change those around us for good and for your glory!

Father, we are plagued by so many things, but they pale in comparison to the persecutions and hardships so many endure around the world! Keep us ever mindful of them! Teach us to do what we can to ease their suffering and pain! Change the hearts and minds of those who persecute them and draw them unto yourself! Thy kingdom come! Thy will be done!

Spread the light of your love to all people! Thy kingdom come! Thy will be done!

Keep us diligent in prayer and in love! Guard our thoughts and actions and being! Love us and lead us!

Pay off our debts that we may freely and generously share our wealth with others! Thy kingdom come! Thy will be done! Love us! Lead us!

In Jesus Name! Amen and amen!

Be thou, our all-in-all!

Dear Dad,

The Day just got away from me, yesterday! Right now, I'm anxious, because I want to do other things. Not into this!

Decided to stay and write! Anxiety is subsiding a bit, but Father, I'm still struggling!

Calming down a bit, Father. Thank you! Bless this day and this week! Help me to get everything together! Help me to not stress over things! Help me to get done what I need to this week and to reach out to people in love and kindness! Thy Kingdom come! Thy will be done! Love us! Lead us!

You are the great God and Father! You are the creator and redeemer of all things! You love us with an everlasting love! With an enduring love! With toughness and gentleness as the situation warrants! Make us like you! Teach us to love and care for one another! To take care of things! To be good stewards of all your marvelous graces! You gift us, that we may gift others!

You are light and life and love and joy and peace! You are our life and livelihood! Apart from you we are nothing and we can do nothing! In you we produce much fruit! Fruit that lasts unto eternity! Fruit that nourishes those around us! Thy Kingdom come! Thy will be done! Love us! Lead us!

Dwell in us and change us from the inside out! Be our confidence and strength! Be our courage and our love! Be thou, our all-in-all! Make us one with you! Make us whole in you!

You are light! Light our way! You are love! Teach us to love! You are life! Enliven us and those around us with your love and mercy and grace!

Let your gentle and powerful Spirit have its way with us to shape and change and purify us! Thy kingdom come! Thy will be done! Love us! Lead us!

Delight in us and be our hearts desire and delight! Prosper us in all things good and helpful! Prosper us and give us grateful and generous hearts, minds, and spirits! Open our hearts! Open our wallets! Let us season others' lives with words and actions of love and kindness and grace! Love us! Lead us and cause us to, joyfully and willingly, follow that lead!

Father, protect us and all people from illness and from all things that come from sin and evil! Work, in all things, for our good and the good of all people! Shower us with your love and protection! Thy kingdom come! Thy will be done!

In Jesus Name! Amen and amen! Thank You!

I do my best to offer you thanks and praise!

Dear Dad,

Can't seem to get motivated to write or work much! Life seems kind of blah and meaningless right now! Tired and bored, I guess! Drifting just drifting!

Oh Father, dear Abba, I will come to you and do my best to offer you thanks and praise! You are the God who gives rest! You are the God who gives wisdom and insight!

Help me to realize, as I sit here in covid camp, bored and anxious and depressed, that there are many others in nursing homes and other places that feel as I do. People that need reassurance and friendship and hope! People that struggle with physical ailments!

You are our light and our life! You are our hope and motivation and delight! You build up! You make new! You renew energy, vitality, and strength! You are the life-giver! You are the hope-bringer! You forgive our sins! You heal all our diseases! You lift up out of the pit! You shower us with good things and renew our youth like the eagle!

You are a great God and Father! You are the faithful redeemer, brother, and friend! Thy Kingdom come! Thy will be done!

You are the life enriching Spirit of love and truth and grace! Thy kingdom come! Thy will be done!

In Jesus name! Amen and amen!

<u>Dragging this morning.</u>

Dear Dad,

Dragging this morning. A front moved through and that may be part of it. I'm pretty well coffeed up this morning and still dragging! Pep me up, please, kind father!

You are the light of the world! You light our path and give us life! True and abundant life in you! We take it for granted! Help us to live in it! To be grateful for it!

Dragging this morning! Bolster my energy, my ambition, and my hope! Help me to get enthused and to do the things I need and would like to do! Give me determination and persistence! Help me to persevere! Give diligence and determination, along with consistency! Let my hope and trust and confidence be in you! Mold me, shape me, use me! Bless and multiply the works of my hand and the words of my mouth!

In you do we hope and trust! You are our light and our life and our being! Dwell in us and help us to abide and dwell in you! Be thou, our joy and delight! Be thou, our fount and source! Be as living water, welling up within us to overflow to those who need your love and encouragement! Thy kingdom come! Thy will be done! In us and through us and round about us as we share your love and goodness and mercy and forgiveness.!

Praying now for _____! Love them! Lead them! Increase your love and mercy in their lives and let them know again the joy of your salvation and love! Thy Kingdom come! Thy will be done!

In Jesus Name! Amen!

Perfect all our words and actions

Dear Dad,
You are the great and loving and patient God and Father! You have dug around me and put on fertilizer year after year! Yet, it seems like my growth has been

slow and my harvest small, at least from my perspective! I ask you, in your mercy, to continue to be patient with me! To continue to water and fertilize me and prune me so that I may produce a rich harvest in you! Make me a productive tree, a fruitful branch!

You are the vine, I, but a branch! Help me to stay connected to you! To find my energy and strength in you! To produce much fruit in you!

You are the great healer! The one who forgives all our sins and heals all our diseases! You are the one who gives vitality and strength! The one who renews our youth and vitality! Strengthen and encourage us! Give us wisdom and energy and strength! Courage and determination and perseverance and hope and faith and trust!

Make me as a youth of 20 again as far as energy and desire goes! Yet make me wise and loving beyond my years! Oh Father, my days are in your keeping! Together let's make them good ones! Thy kingdom come! Thy will be done!

Father extend my days for mercy sake and let the glory and productivity of my later days exceed that of my former! Do a new thing within me and make me fruitful and productive in you! Guard and protect me from the evil one and all his tricks! Let my trust be in you! Make us wise and generous, caring, and compassionate!

Perfect all our words and actions, through your Son and the work of your good Spirit! Help us to remember that he completes what is lacking in us and makes us "new" and "perfect" and "good enough" in him! Come, Lord Jesus, come, and in your perfect timing make all things new in you! Come, Holy Spirit, continue to change us and shape us and bless and use us!

In Jesus Name! Amen and Amen!

Three strand cord of light and life and love!

Dear Dad,

You are a great God! Thanks for a great week! Not too much I wanted to say this morning, I guess, except thanks for getting me back on track! Come, Jesus, Come! Come, Holy Spirit, come!

Come in perfect timing and power to transform! To enlighten! To encourage and to cause me to act! Make my "Why" loud within me! Be thou, my "Why" and my heart's desire!

I love you, Holy Trinity! The Great One! Three strand cord of light and life and love! Let us live and move and have our being in You! Make us one!

Amen and Amen!

Guard us this day from harm and danger and cause us to flee from all temptation and sin!

In Jesus Name Amen!

Mysteries of the ages unfolding before our eyes!

Dear Dad,

Your mercies are new every morning! They sustain us and uplift and encourage us throughout the day!

You are a great God! Loving and caring, all knowing, with our eternal best interests at heart!

You lift up! You sustain and prosper and make whole and one in you! Teach us to abide in you and to bear much fruit in you! Teach us to invest our lives with an eternal return in mind! Send us as reapers in your harvest of righteousness and souls, gathering all that has been broken down and scattered, so that nothing may be lost or wasted!

You have sowed good seed into us, now at your good coming sort out and destroy and purify us from every evil and unhelpful thing!

Mold us shape us! Refine us, that we may be living vessels of your love and care!

You are God of God and light of Light! Very God of Very God! Father and brother Savior and friend and Spirit of life and truth, mercy and justice, love and joy and peace!

Fill us and transform us from the inside out! Oh, fount and source! Oh, living-one, whose existence is of old even from eternity and everlasting to everlasting!

You are the source and cause of all that exists! You think it and speak it and it is ordained and accomplished in the heavens and on earth!

Oh, Christ brother and friend, savior in whom we trust and depend! Oh, comforter and confronter of the truth! You are the way, the truth, and the life and through you we have access to the Father! You are the restorer of all things! You make new again so that nothing can overcome it! You have put sin and death under your feet and given us life in abundance and fullness!

Make us partakers of that life! Cause us to think and act and live so that many others may know you and the life you give!

Heal us in an instant and in eternity! Heal us in mind body and spirit and make us new and one in you and in the Father, the great "I AM" of body and soul, even Yahweh of old!

Yahweh saves! Blessed be the name of Yahweh and of His son, the chosen and anointed one, who does his bidding and brings all things to pass! Our light and life and the fullness of joy and peace!

In you do the nations hope and put their trust! Let all the peoples praise you, oh God! Let all your holy people bring you offerings of thanksgiving and praise!

When they see you coming in the clouds, when they faint and fall to the ground in fear and trembling, then speak to them your words of comfort and care and repent their hearts of stone! Give them new hearts of love and mercy and truth! When they come to their senses let them proclaim, "Yahweh Saves!" and let them return to their Father with rejoicing and singing and much laughter and joy.

Let them bring offerings of thanksgiving and praise saying, "Jesus! Jesus! Yahweh Saves! Blessed be the Name of Yahweh and of His Holy One who leads us home! Who prepares a place for us in Him for eternity and makes us one!

Oh, revelation upon revelation, mysteries of the ages unfolding before our eyes! Our hearts and our minds cannot contain it! We break into singing with much rejoicing and laughter and joy!

He wipes every tear from our eyes and even our tears of relief and joy he turns into laughter and dancing and singing!

Let all the world rejoice! Let people from the ends of the earth and beyond and all the companies of the heavens in dimensions beyond dimensions and in

worlds unknown rejoice! Let all the people and all creation bring you their unending thanks and praise!

In your perfect timing you acted mightily through
your Son to redeem and save and make new! Come
Yahweh. Come! Come, oh Lamb of God, come! Come,
Holy Spirit come! And in your perfect timing make us
and all things new!

Amen and amen! In Jesus Name, Amen!

Break down the barrier wall that separates

Oh God, our days are in your keeping, whether they
are long or short on this earth, they are in your hands!
Guard us and protect us from temptation and evil!

Give us, this day, those things we need to support
body and soul and spirit and give us an overflowing
abundance to share with others!

Forgive us and teach us to forgive! Help us in our
un-forgiveness! Thy kingdom come! Thy will be done
in us and through us and round about us that on earth
and in the heaven your name may be hallowed and
blessed and all your people may be one in you and in
your Son!

Break down the barrier wall that separates people
from people and ourselves from all you would have us
to be!

Amen and amen! Come quickly and in your perfect
timing! Amen and amen! In Jesus Name, Amen!

That's how it is with pet sins

Dear Dad,

I blew it again yesterday and not even sure I'm sorry. Not sure there is anything to be sorry for! I am sorry but in the heat of the moment, I feel powerless to stop and even want to!

That's how it is with pet sins like overeating! We all have them. Things we don't even want to call sin! Things we enjoy doing, but which are probably not helpful for us or others in the long run!

Forgive me! After saying that for the umpteenth time and knowing that I will probably fall again it sounds very hollow! I'm not sure my heart is in it or that I am sincere, but what else can I say?

You are light and life and mercy and justice! I must turn back to you for there is no one else! No place else where hope can be found!

So, forgive me! Renew me set me back on your path for me! Give plan and purpose to my life and help me to follow it! To cherish it and to live it! Thy kingdom come! Thy will be done!

Amen and amen! In Jesus Name, amen!

Move us and motivate us by your great love and mercy!

Dear Abba,

Let my hope and my trust be in you! I do trust you; help my unbelief! I do hope, for hope can be found nowhere else!

Light of light and love! God who brings joy and laughter from sorrow and pain! Love us and lead us! Cause us to bless your name and to do your will! Thy kingdom come! Thy will be done!

You love us with an everlasting love! You parent us as we need! Your greatest desire is to see us home safe with you for eternity! Change our hearts and minds to love you and each other as we should! Thy kingdom come! Thy will be done! Love us, lead us, and cause us to willingly and joyfully follow you!

Father we often sin and fall short, but in you there is forgiveness and newness of life and hope and joy and peace in the journey! We are disobedient children, unworthy and unfaithful servants and stewards of your grace and mercy!

Cause to love and live aright! Move us and motivate us by your great love and mercy! Cover us in the righteousness of your Son! Provide wedding garments for us and cause us to gladly wear them at the wedding feast of the Lamb, your Son, our Savior and brother and friend! The one who sits at your right hand! The one who is the way, the truth, and the life! One with the Father and the Spirit!

Dwell in us and cause us to dwell and abide in you and bear much fruit! A rich harvest! Thy kingdom come! Thy will be done!

Provide, for us, day by day, all that we need to support this body and life! Care for our mind, body, emotions, and spirit! Guard us from evil and help us to turn from temptation!

You are the way, the truth, and the life! The great "I Am" in whom we live and move and have our being! Apart from you we cease to exist! You are light and life! Help us to dwell in you! To abide in You!

In Jesus name! Amen and Amen!

Often, we try to shortcut things!

Thank you, Dear Father, for another day! Help me to live it wisely and with love!

You are our God and Father! You are the creator and sustainer of all things! You alone give light and life! In you we exist and have our being! You are light and life and love! In you do we hope! In you do we trust! Help us to trust you fully! Trust you in all areas of our lives! Give us wisdom, and hope and faith and love as we live out our lives!

Father, often, we stumble and fall! Often, we try to shortcut things! Often, we do not trust you fully! Put away and remove from us all things that cause us to become entangled in sin and doubt! Increase our faith and trust in you! Remove fear and doubt and help us to move forward in faith, with humility and courage! Thy Kingdom come! Thy will be done! In Jesus Name! Amen!

Give us, Godly delays!

Dear Dad,

Just had some trouble with my computer booting up. It kept sitting on a blank screen. Finally got it to turn off and then on again. I was a little frustrated with the delay and then I thought what if that short delay kept me from being involved in a traffic accident later in the morning, because I was running just a little late, or even something as simple as giving me the time to remember something I had forgotten.

Oh God, how you redeem our time not letting any of it be wasted but using it and working it out for our good and the good of others!

I know I wouldn't have thought about all this if it were it not for the delay this morning! Give us, Godly delays! Slow us down to remember you and others!

You are a great God! You are the keeper of our days! You hold eternity in your hands! Nothing escapes your notice! You work all things out for our eternal good!

God of God, light of light, even very God of very God, You are amazing! We don't always understand your ways but we have glimpsed enough of your working in our lives that we know you are good! We know you have the best interest in mind for our lives and the lives of others! What seems meaningless and wasted to us, you claim as your own and use it!

You redeem time and space! You work evil out for good! You take what seems permanent and final, even death itself, and you laugh and make new and resurrect and transform, saying, "See the abundance of my children!" I have made them new in the blood of the Lamb! Sin and death have no hold on them! They come to me freely, to worship and give thanks and praise! See how they love me and one another! How justice and mercy flow like a life-giving river!"

You are a great God, above all gods! Creator and sustainer and redeemer of all things! Holy Father, friend, and Savior, and brother, life giving life transforming life, renewing Spirit! You are the source of all good things! Incomprehensible three-in-one, living, creative, transforming, word become flesh for our sake and for the sake of all created beings!

Mold us! Shape us! Cause us to dream dreams and see visions and prophesy rightly, in your name.! Cause us not to be elated by revelation, but to walk humbly and courageously with you!

Guard our steps, our thoughts, words, and actions! Redeem our time and order our days that we and many others may spend eternity in oneness with you, with your Son and with each other! Love us lead us, dear God! Great "I AM!" Yahweh of old! Father God! Daddy God! Abba Father!

Our minds get carried away with trying to know you and understand you and comprehend you! Set us back on the firm foundation of your love! Give us humble spirits that acknowledge that all we are and can do are but gifts and trusts from you! Make us good stewards, faithful servants of your grace and love and mercy, that trusting in You, we might have an eternal inheritance as your beloved children of light and love!

Teach us! Mold us! Shape us! Make us of use and value to you and each other, in this world and the next! Give eternal plan and purpose and significance and meaning to our earthly existence! Thy kingdom come! Thy will be done, on earth as in the heavens!

Provide for all our needs of body and soul and remind us that you are the one thing needful, that truly in you do we live and move and have our purpose and being! Guard us from temptation and evil! Forgive our sins and open our hearts to forgive and love each other! Breakdown the walls that separate and divide and make us one in you, one in your Son! Let us proclaim his name saying, "Yahweh Saves!"

Blessed be, Yahweh., God of God and God of light and life and purpose and being, who created us to be in union with Himself, to enjoy fellowship and communion and community and oneness with Him!

Redeem and transform us in your perfect timing. In the fullness of time and beyond act to make all things new in you and in your Son!

Abba Father. Daddy God, brother Jesus, go with us this day and lead us by the power and action of your good Spirit within us! Love us! Lead us!

Transform our hearts and soul and minds that we may love you and trust you with all our being and strength!

You are a great God, Father of all the living! Bless now this day, multiply our acts of kindness and love, blessing them with an eternal abundance of righteousness and souls! Forgive our sins and transform and use even them to work things out for our good and the eternal wellbeing of others! Redeem order and number our days in your wisdom and love! Thy Kingdom come and Thy Will be done among us and in us and through us, today and forever without end!

Amen and Amen and Amen, In Jesus' strong name we pray! Come quickly and in your perfect timing! Amen!

Forgive me father for wallowing in sin and despair.

Dear Dad,

Tired this morning. Thank you for the nice weather the last few days. I have things to do and I can feel tension and anxiety starting to rise. Quell my fear and anxiety! Still my anxious heart and mind! Fill me with courage and determination and desire! Equip and encourage me and empower and lead me! Thy kingdom come! Thy will be done! Love us and lead us!

Not much into this this morning! Forgive me father for wallowing in sin and despair. Lift me out of the pit! Let me sing songs of thanksgiving and praise to you! Let me type out my thanksgiving and praise on the keys of my computer!

You are loving and kind! You give courage and strength! Ambition and motivation! In you is plan and purpose! In you is joy and life and hope! You raise up! You make new! In you do we hope! In you will we trust! Thy kingdom come! Thy will be done! Love us! Lead us!

Great God and Father, faithful brother and Savior and friend, Savior and Lord, good and life-giving Spirit, dwell in us and make us new! Make us one in you! Make us whole in you! Teach us to walk humbly yet courageously with you! God of God and very God of Very God, fount and source and sustainer of all good things, enlighten encourage and empower us with wisdom, determination, courage, and hope and love! Provide an abundance of all your good gifts and help us to share with grateful, willing, and generous hearts minds and spirits! Thy kingdom come! Thy will be done! Love us! Lead us!

Delight in us and cause us to delight in you! Go with us this day and strengthen and guide us in the ways we should go.

Amen and amen! In Jesus name, amen!

Father God, feeling out of it this morning.

Dear Dad,

Father God, feeling out of it this morning. Hard to draw near to you. Forgive my sins! Comfort and confront me in love as only you can! Turn my heart and mind back to you! Help me to shed every sin and shortcoming that drags me down!

You, Oh God, forgive all our sins! Forgive us and renew us! You heal all our diseases! Heal us! You renew our energy, and courage and strength! Renew us and make us fruitful in you! In Jesus name Amen!

Take away the love of sinning!

Dear Dad,
A little tired this morning. Still coffeeing-up. Stomach is a little funny.

Father God, You are our health and our strength! Our healer and deliverer! You forgive all our sins! You heal all our diseases! You shower us with good things! You renew our youth and vitality! You are the great healer of body, soul, and spirit! You build up and You tear down, so you can build better in its place!

Mold us! Shape us! Heal us! Use us! Father, we are sinners! Too often we have fallen short of our potential, too often we have become entangled by our shortcomings, bad habits, and sins. Take away the love of sinning! By your good Spirit make us new and holy and one!

Take away my idolatry to food and replace it with moderation and gratitude! Help me to manage myself well! Help me to delay gratification in favor of better healthier things in the long run.

Give us grateful hearts that share all your good gifts with others! Thy kingdom come! Thy will be done!

Praying now for Family and friends. For _____, and _____, and _____, and _____, and all my family and friends! Draw them unto yourself! Let their hope and their trust be in you! Thy Kingdom come! Thy will be done!

Go with us this day! Together let's make it a good one! Bless this day and all in it!

In Jesus Name! Amen and Amen!

<u>Teach us to hold very loosely to the things of this world</u>

Dear Dad,

It's thanksgiving and we have so much to be thankful for. Thank you for everything. Thank you for our new home and for our family. Bless us and keep us and make us a blessing.

Father, we are so blessed! Teach us to bless others! Teach us to hold very loosely to the things of this world for they are fleeting! Teach us that you are the one thing needful! You are our fount and source and sustainer! Help us to learn to trust you and to look to you for all things! Lead us, love us, and cause us to learn and grow in you!

You are the abundant life-giver. The thief comes to kill, steal, and destroy but You give life eternally in abundance! Make us rich in all things helpful, that we might enrich the lives of others! That we might share with them that you are the one thing needful!

Mold us! Make us! Shape us! Pay off our debts and fill us to overflowing with an abundance of your richest blessings! As it is your will and in our best interest and in the eternal benefit of others, give us long life on this earth, rich days full of love and joy! We pray not our will but thine, be done, for you truly have our best and eternal interest at heart!

We are often selfish and short sighted! Increase our generosity, increase our vision, and our hope and our trust in you! Fill us with your life-giving, life-changing presence! Lead us in the paths we should go! Do more than we can think, or dream, or imagine.! Thy will be done, thy kingdom come in us and through us and round about us!

Order our day and our ways! Set right and true hearts and minds within us! Teach us to look to you as the source of all good things! Teach us to look to you as the one who brings abundant light and life and love to us even in the face of disaster!

Transform us and fill us! Make us one in you! Let us abide and bear much fruit, a rich harvest of right-eousness and souls! Love us! Lead us! Mold us! Make us and transform us, good Father!

Light and love, life-giver and sustainer, we give you thanks and praise for your abundant mercies and bless-ings! We pray for those with needs of body and soul! Teach us what we can do and empower us to act, to share your love and goodness and mercy!

Amen and Amen and Amen in Jesus Name, Amen!

Bless the Lord, oh my soul!

Bless the Lord, oh my soul! Bless the lord and forget not all his benefits! It is he who forgives all our sins! It is he who heals all our diseases! It is he who lifts us up out of the pit! It is he who crowns us with steadfast love and mercy! It is he who gives us good things and renews our youth like the eagles!

Bless the Lord, oh my soul! All you peoples, bless the Lord, the great God, Yahweh! He is the great "I Am" of old, source of health and wealth and strength! He is full of forgiveness and compassion and healing!

Bless the Lord, all you lands! Come to the God, Yahweh! Come from the east and from the west and bless his holy name! Revere his Son, the faithful one, our righteousness and our help! Friend and Savior and brother! The crucified one who died and rose! The resurrected one who gives life in his name, proclaiming "Yahweh saves!"

Blessed be the name of Yahweh! Return to Yahweh, your help and your health and your salvation! The one "who is and was and is to come!" The eternal one in whom there is light and life, hope and power and purpose and being! Dwell in Him and let His good Spirit dwell in you!

Absorb the power of his word and proclaim it to the nations! Yes, absorb the power and forgiveness of his Son, the begotten one, the word become flesh for our sake and for the sake of all people! The very lamb of God! The anointed one! The lion of Judah! The humble and courageous shepherd of the sheep! The living one, who gives life and health to dead bones!

Praise the Lord, of my soul! Bless his holy name! Live and move and have your being in him! Find your health and your strength and your motivation and energy in Him! Make Him your heart's delight! Your all-in-all! Your hope and your courage and strength and peace when things are hard! Your joy and delight when he redeems you and fills your life with blessing!

Bless the Lord, oh my soul and forget not His benefits! He is your health and salvation! He is your joy and your strength! He is your health and your wealth! In Him, do the nations rejoice! In Him, do all people find salvation, forgiveness, and rest!

Praise the Lord, oh my soul! Bless his holy name!

You are light and life!

Dear Dad,

Thank you for another day in this place! Help us to make it a good one!

You are light and life! You are the light and love of the world! You make new and holy and one! You are our light and salvation! You are our deliverer and our strength! Thy kingdom come! Thy will be done!

Light of all goodness and strength! Giver of all good gifts! You forgive all our sins! You heal all our diseases! You lift us up out of the pit of destruction and despair! You renew our youth and vitality and ambition! Thy Kingdom come! Thy will be done! Love us! Lead us!

Delight in us and cause us to delight in you! Be, thou the desire and delight of our heart and mind! Thy kingdom come! Thy will be done!

In Jesus Name, Amen and Amen!

You enter into our world as flesh and blood for our sake!

Dear Dad,

Didn't sleep very well last night. I ached and I was worried about stuff.

You, oh God, are light and life! You are the energy and being and oneness in which we all have our being! In you do we find plan and purpose and hope! In you do we find courage and motivation and strength!

You love us with an enduring, relentless, everlasting, love! Our minds boggle when we try and understand you! We cannot comprehend your goodness and glory and being!

We are humbled by your presence and all our best qualities and talents pale in comparison with You! Yet. you have filled us with the presence of your good Spirit! You anointed us with courage and power, abilities and authority, from on high! We go in your name and in the name of your Son proclaiming, "Yahweh Saves! Blessed be the name of Yahweh!" Thy kingdom come! Thy will be done!

How can we thank you for your love and tender mercies? What words can proclaim your goodness and mercy and glory? You are the greatest and best! The only one in whom all things hold together! Light of light and love of love, everlasting of everlasting! You transcend time and space! And yet, you enter into it as flesh and blood for our sake!

Teach us and enable us to walk humbly, yet boldly and courageously with you! To walk in the full authority of your Son! Let us teach and heal and raise from the dead in Jesus' name and in the power of His death and resurrection which covers our sin and makes new and holy!

You make us your precious children! You give us rank and ability and authority far beyond what we often realize, use, or accept! We are unworthy servants, disobedient children!

Change our hearts and minds! Set us back on a right path! Hear us not for our many words, rather use them to remind us of your great goodness and power and mercy! Thy kingdom come! Thy will be done!

In Jesus' Name, Amen and amen!

Be thou the delight and desire of our hearts!

Father God, life-giving and sustain Spirit of transformation and mercy, dearest Jesus, Savior, redeemer and brother and friend, you are a great God! You are the only true God. We can only begin to comprehend you and your works and your ways! Thy Kingdom come! Thy will be done!

Light of life and love, source of all goodness and mercy, courage and strength, delight in us and be thou the delight and desire of our hearts! Too often we stray! Draw us back to you and restore to us the joy of your salvation! Dwell in us and transform us and teach us to walk humbly and courageously with you! Light our way! Be a voice beside us and behind us and in front of us, whispering go this way! Lead us! Love us!

Help us to live as your beloved children of light and love and mercy and truth! You are the way, the truth, and the life! In you is hope and plan and purpose and being! In you is true life! Go with us this day and lead us in the way we should go!

Amen and Amen! In Jesus Name!

Having you alone is abundantly enough!

Dear Dad,

I was down sick with a stomach bug yesterday! Hard to give thanks and praise to you when you feel miserable, but I did my best knowing that you work all things out for good!

How transient is our existence on this planet! How short are our days! But you, oh God, have set eternity in our hearts! In you do we trust.! Teach us to order our days aright! Teach us to focus on you and serving and helping others! Teach us to be heavenly-minded, trusting that when our days here are ended you have even more glorious things in store!

You are God and Father, the fount and source of all light and life and goodness! You bring life and health, joy and peace and love! In you we find our plan and purpose! In you we live and move and have our being!

Give us contented, yet courageous hearts! Hearts that are contented with what we have, knowing that having you alone is abundantly enough! Yet, hearts that seek good things for ourselves and others!

Let justice and mercy and love and goodness flow in us and through us with abundance. Prosper and flourish us with all things good and helpful to us and others! Let goodness and light and life increase even in the midst of a darkening world! Let not our love grow cold! Instead let it shine ever brighter in this dark place! Give us ever gratefull and thankful hearts and minds!

You are a great God! A God of abundance and mercy and love and grace! Instruct us in your ways and cause us to follow! You are light and life and love! Help us to reflect that to the world.!

Amen and amen! In Jesus Name, Amen!

Help us to remember that it is all yours anyway!

Dear Dad,

Yawning this morning! Yet, I had 7 hours of the best sleep I've had lately! Slept most of the night except for getting up to go to the bathroom. Still getting used to mornings without coffee, but we'll get through it. It's thanksgiving! Thank you!

Father God, you have given us so much and blessed us greatly throughout the years, help us to be grateful and generous in return! Help us to remember that it is all yours anyway! You are the master of the house we are but your children and servants!

You love us with an everlasting love! You create! You redeem! You rescue! You buy back! You make new! You make holy! You make one!

Let us find our being and oneness in you! Let us abide with you, as you dwell in us, to mold and shape and transform! You love us with an endearing love, an enduring love, an everlasting love!

You are our hope! You are our joy! You are our rest, our peace, our shalom! Love us and lead us!

In Jesus name! Amen!

Let me seek you and find you

Dear Dad,

You, oh God, are merciful and kind! Filled with compassion and loving mercy! You are the light of the world! The way, the truth, and the life!

Let me seek you and find you and walk with you, all my days in this place! Thy kingdom come! Thy will be done! Love us and lead us gracious Lord and father!

In Jesus name amen!

Yet in my boldness as your little child

Dear Dad,

Not sure I truly know what it means that I am your child! Not sure I grasp all the privileges, blessings, freedoms, and responsibilities! I know however, though sometimes I doubt, that you love me!

Forgive me and engulf me in your love! Let me know that I can trust you fully! Let me know that you have the best interest of me and all your children in your heart and mind! Let me know that you work for good in all things!

You are my dad, my daddy, my dear abba, my counselor, and defense, my healer and my friend! You are the one I run to with my joys and with my fears!

Still, sometimes though, I am afraid of you! Your justice and your righteousness cause me to fear for I am a sinner and unholy! Yet in your love and great mercy, and for the sake of your Son, I am not afraid to come into your presence! Help me to not take your great love for granted!

Father, your blessings are too numerous to count! Family and friends! Home and food, cars and, computers, and all this world's blessings and goods! Love, joy, peace, acceptance, courage and patience and faith and so many more spiritual blessings and gifts!

Father, as I look at my needs. I notice that I still struggle sometimes in stepping out in courage and faith! There are probably many other areas I don't even recognize now, but those are the ones that come to mind!

Grant courage and faith in abundance! Help me to know that I can step out in courage and faith asking and expecting your blessing on my efforts! Knowing and believing that you can do more than I can think or ask or imagine!

Help me to step out in faith and wait and trust you for the results! Help me to believe that you are using and blessing and multiplying my efforts, even if I cannot see it, or even if they seem to have failed! Love me! Lead me!

We give you thanks and praise for your patience with us! For the trust you have placed in us! For the multiple ways you have worked in our lives! For blessing and using our sometimes meager and even begrudging efforts! For encouraging us to step out in faith! To trust you no matter what comes!

Father, our days are in your keeping! You have already blessed me and extended my days beyond what I deserve! Yet in my boldness as your little child, I ask that you extend them further and fill me with courage and faith and action that I may be your faithful servant and child! I pray all this asking that thy will be done and that thy kingdom would come through it!

My days are in your hands! Let my trust and hope be in you! In Jesus name! Amen and Amen!

Got a load of laundry in and it was kind of a struggle.

Dear Dad,

Dragging this morning. Got a load of laundry in and it was kind of a struggle. Seems like I slept much of the day yesterday.

Father God, coffee is starting to kick in, maybe. Starting to feel a little better. Not really feeling into this this morning, but here goes!

You are the God of life! You are the God of health and vitality and strength and joy! In you do we hope! In you do we trust!

You are my refuge and my strength! You are the righteous and holy one! You make new! You give life! You forgive all our sins! You heal all our diseases! You rescue us from destruction and despair! You lift us out of the pit and set us on the solid ground of your Son, our Savior and brother and friend!

You give life! You make new! You restore vitality, motivation, and strength! You light our way! You set us on the good path! You call us and lead us by the hand! You are always with us! You are our light and our life! You give plan and purpose to our being! You are the light of the world and of every living being! In you will we trust! In you will we hope and trust! Thy kingdom come! Thy will be done!

Go with us this day! Strengthen and encourage us! And keep us! In Jesus Name, we pray!

Change us into your children of light and love!

Father, we are so blessed! Thank you! Make us a blessing to others!

You are God and Father! You are light and life! You are the way-maker! You are the way and truth and life!

You make new! You make holy and one! Dwell in us and change us into your children of light and love!

You are God of God! You are the only true God! You light our way! You redeemed us and bought us back from sin and death and evil!

You keep us safe from the evil one! You shower us with good gifts! You renew our strength and hope! You give us generous and compassionate hearts and minds!

You are the light and life of the world! In you we live and move and have our being! In you we find plan and purpose for our existence! You are our light and our life!

Guard and keep us and help us to follow.

In Jesus name! Amen and Amen!

Look at Maddie, your precious little child

Dear Dad,

Your mercies are new every morning! They are fresh with the dawn! With every breath I take, you bless and strengthen the inner person! Even if our bodies fail and wither, yet you sustain us! None is like you in love and mercy and forgiveness.! You desire good things for your people! You transform us into beings of light and laughter and love!

Look at Maddie, your precious little child, full of laughter and love! Full of hope! Full of You! May we be like her in all the best ways! May we come to you and love you and trust you! May we love and laugh

with you and those around us! You are full of grace!
Love us! Lead us!

Lead us! Guide us that we do not fall into temptation
or sin and help us to pay my debts and serve others!

Love us and lead us, this day and always!

Amen and Amen! In Jesus, Name Amen!

Help us to embrace fully the life that is your Son!

Dear Dad,

Thy kingdom come! Thy will be done! Love us and
lead us, Father of light and life and love! Help us to
walk in the way that is your Son! Help us to love and
believe and follow the truth that is your Son! Help us
to embrace fully the life that is your Son, by the power
of your good Spirit at work within us! Thy Kingdom
come! Thy will be done!

In Jesus Name! Amen!

Let us give hope and joy to the nations!

Dear Dad,

Your mercies are new every morning! Give us grateful and receptive hearts that we may receive all you
would pour into us! Open our heart and minds! Give
faith and trust and belief in abundance!

You are light and life! In you do the people hope!
In you do, I hope! Let also my trust be in you! Praying for a friend this morning! Heal her and draw her
unto you and unto your Son!

Father God, brother Jesus, life-giving Spirit, You
forgive our Sins! You heal all our diseases! You com-

fort and convict! You make new and holy in and through your Son! You raise us up out of the pit! You crown our lives with good things! You renew our hope and strength! You renew our youth, like the eagles!

Father God, blessed abba, Yahweh of old, Yeshua in whom we hope, blessed Spirit of light and life! I am still a babe in my understanding! Grow me in the ways I need to grow and give me firm unswerving childlike faith!

Forgive me, Father, for I am a doubter and a skeptic from way back! I think once I trusted you! I think once you were my source and delight, my hope and courage and strength! Be thou all that again!

You are my hope! You are my strength and my courage from day to day! You are my Father-God. my dear abba Father! My big brother and savior and friend! In you do I hope! In you do I trust! With you, I will walk humbly and with you I will do great things, even miracles beyond my belief and ability! For you are the God who blesses our humble efforts! You are the one who blesses our bold proclamations! You speak and it comes to pass and you have given that authority to your children, even unto me!

Guard our words! Let us speak words of blessing and hope and healing, in your name and in the name of your Son, the anointed one, the risen one! Thy kingdom come mightily upon us! Thy will be done boldly through us!

Let us loose the chains of the captives! Let us give hope and joy to the nations! Replace fear and anxiety and worry with your courage and your strength! In you do we trust! Help our unbelief and let us not be discouraged or dismayed!

For the Spirit of the Yahweh Almighty is upon us, because the He has anointed us to proclaim good news to the poor! He has sent us to bind up the brokenhearted, to proclaim freedom to the captives and to release the prisoners from darkness! He has sent us to proclaim the year of the His goodness and the day of His vengeance on all His enemies! He has sent us to comfort all who mourn and provide for those who grieve and cry! To give them a crown of beauty and honor instead of dust and ashes, the oil of gladness and joy instead of mourning and loud lamenting, and to bestow on them a garment of thanksgiving and praise instead of a spirit of depression and despair! They will be called strong trees of righteousness and goodness and blessing, a planting of Yahweh to display his glory and splendor. (Isaiah 61:1-3 Paraphrased)

Time to be about your work, dear Father! Time to heal and set free and make new! To do the work of your Son, to be like him! Father God, let us share in the ministry of your son, let us call to repentance, let us proclaim the kingdom of God, let us heal and set free, let us forgive sins, and raise from the dead!

We are all dead in our sins but through your Son, you make us alive again! You give us rich and full and abundant life in your Son by the power of your good Spirit!

Increase our faith! Let our trust be in you! Open our hearts and minds and ears to hear you and to follow your lead! Thy Kingdom come! Thy will be done!

Amen and Amen! In Jesus Name!

Knead into me the leaven of love and justice and mercy

Dear Dad,

I can feel the anxiety coming back! Teach me to trust you. To love you! To find joy and hope and wisdom and truth and knowledge and love in you! You are my source and sustainer and strength! My rock and sure defense! My light and my life from day to day!

Yet, so often, I forget you and go my own way! Hear me for your namesake! Hold me and help me and cause me to love you and all people! Give me your heart and your mind and your Spirit!

Teach me your ways! Make me new in you! Refine me as Gold or Silver! Knead into me the leaven of love and justice and mercy until they have their full effect in transforming me into your likeness, oh bread of heaven! Help me to dream, your dreams and to put them into action!

You are God of God, Light of Life! We praise and thank you for your transforming presence! Lead us and love us and cause us to be one in you and with each other!

Give us grateful, wise, obedient, and generous, hearts, minds, and spirits. Cause us to be your people, true children of our heavenly Father! Come, Lord Jesus, come! Come life-giving, life-transforming Spirit! Come, Father God, dwell with us, and in us and round about us.! Let your all-encompassing presence give us life and love and hope and joy! Let us live and move and have our being in you!

Amen and Amen and Amen! In Jesus Name! Amen!

You make the difficult, easy, the impossible possible and probable!

Dear Dad,

You, oh Father, are the light of my life and my being! In you do I live and move and have my being! In you do I take refuge! In you do I delight! In you do I laugh and dance and sing joyful songs!

You lift up! You make new! You make the difficult, easy, the impossible possible and probable! You resurrect and save! You heal all our diseases! You lift us up out of the pit! You forgive all our sins! You crown us with love and compassion and mercy!

You are the light and life of the world! My heart leaps for joy at your name! You give life and light and being! Plan and purpose! You feed us with good things! You walk with us and get us through hard and difficult times! You want the best for us! You know us better than we know ourselves! Thy kingdom come! Thy will be done!

Love us and lead us, gracious Lord and Father, Savior and Spirit, brother and friend! Thy Kingdom come! Thy will be done!

Go with us this day! Lead us and encourage us in the way we should go! Light of Life and all goodness and courage, love, and strength be our source and our guide!

In Jesus Name! Amen and Amen!

Overcome the darkness within and without!

Dear daddy God, dear abba Father, savior and brother and friend and Lord! Thy kingdom come! Thy will be done!

Dwell in us and support and sustain us in body, mind, and spirit! Bring light and life to our souls! Enrich and enliven our being! Let us see and experience good things from you! Let pain and sorrow and sadness and fear have no dominion within us! Instead, let us spread liberally, your joy and peace and healing, along with all good things and the message of your kingdom of light and love! Thy kingdom come! Thy will be done! Love us! Lead us!

Light of love, overcome the darkness within and without! Love us and lead us in Jesus name! Give us hope and courage and perseverance to get through the hard times! Thy kingdom come! Thy will be done!

You are our healer and our strength! Our life and our light! Love us as only you can! Transform us as only you can!

In an instant or in the fullness of time, little by little make us new and whole and holy and one in you and in your Son by the power of your good Spirit! Give us wise generous and loving hearts! Thy kingdom come! Thy will be done! Love us! Lead us!

In in Jesus name! Amen

YAHWEH SAVES!

Bless the Lord, oh my Soul! Bless Yahweh the great I Am.! Bless Him and praise his name! For it is He who forgives all your sins! He who heals all your diseases! He who gives light and life and redeems you from the pit of destruction! It is he who satisfies your longings with good things and renews your youth, day by day so that you can do things once thought impossible!

Yes, bless Yahweh, oh my soul! Bless Him and praise Him and thank Him! Walk with Him and revere Him! Draw near to Him, for He has drawn near to us! He has given us his very Spirit to dwell within us!

In Him we live and move and have our being! Apart from him we can do no good thing! Praise the Lord, Yahweh, oh my soul! Bless Him and thank and praise Him for His great goodness and glory!

Praise Him for His merciful and benevolent kingdom, that He has brought near to us and placed within us that we might walk humbly and courageously with Him, spreading His love and healing, and sharing the great good news that God is near to all who repent and believe and call upon His name!

His name is love and light and hope and joy and peace! His name is shalom and all things find their plan and purpose and being in Him!

Yes, bless Yahweh, all you people! Proclaim YAHWEH SAVES! Trust in Him! Find your light and life and being in Him for they come from no other!

The thief come to kill, steal, and destroy! But Yahweh Saves! He has come that we might have life in Him! Even the fullness of life, with all joy and gladness and hope and peace!

Bless Yahweh, oh my soul and bless his Son whose very name proclaims, "Yahweh Saves!"

Amen and Amen! Jesus' name we proclaim and in that name we pray! Amen and Amen!

Out of my depths shall I sing forth hosannas and hallelujahs!

Dear Dad,

You are great! You are grand, and my heart just isn't into thanking and praising you this morning! Sorry!

I had a meltdown yesterday and wound up the afternoon very irritable! This morning I'm dragging! I've had coffee and been back to bed a couple of times, but no help!

Revive me, oh God! Fill me with your words! Encourage me and set me back on the path of joy and hope in You!

You are a great God, worthy of thanks and praise! Therefore, I praise you and give you thanks!

Out of my depths shall I sing forth hosannas and hallelujahs! From the pit I will call out to my God, who rescues and saves! Who provides my soul with good things! Who turns disaster and mourning into blessing upon blessing!

You restore life and fortunes! You lift up so that no one can drag us down again! You cast out sin and death and sickness along with every evil and harmful thing!

Come quickly, to rescue and save, that my mouth may give unending thanks and praise!

In the morning let me thank you and praise you for a new day fresh with your mercies and love! At noon may I pause to bring you thanksgiving and praise! As you close my eyes in sleep, let my last words be, thank you, God!

Thank you, Father God, Brother Jesus, life giving Spirit! Thank you for keeping me this day and bless me through the dark night!

You are the God who goes with His people to give courage and wisdom, counsel and strength! You are the God, who dares to dwell within your people, "Saying abide in me and I will abide in you!" You are the God who comes to us and makes us one!

Come, Father God! Come, brother and savior and friend! Come transforming Spirit of life and truth and grace! Come and abide with us! Dwell in us and become such a part of us that sin and evil, doubt and fear have no place in our lives! Dwell in us and above us, under and around us! Let us move and have our purpose and being in you! Light of light! Very God of Very God! The great "I AM!" The source and sustainer of all things, of every good and perfect thing!

Dwell in us and make us perfect in you! Dwell in us and justify us and redeem us from all unrighteousness! Love us and lead us and make us new in You!

We have things to do and places to go! Go with us and help us to follow your lead!

Amen and Amen! In Jesus name, amen!

Today is a day of feasting and fasting!

Dear Dad,
Struggling again this morning! I am OK though, for you are with me! Your rod and your staff, they comfort me! You lead and guide and encourage me saying, "Be strong! Be not afraid! I and all my hosts are with you! You have at your disposal all the resources of the universe! You have full access to the creator and sustainer

of all things! Go in peace and love and joy! Go in boldness and humility and power and courage and strength! Depression has no hold on you! Behold today and tomorrow and forever, I set you free! I am God of Gods, Lord of Lords! I set things in action and cause them to be! Buy a lottery ticket! Put me to the test! Whether you win or lose I am with you! I will work it out for good! You are already a winner in my book! Do you need a million or two or 50 or 500 million or a billion? Name it and I will give it! I gave my Son what will I withhold from you? Yet, not all things are helpful, perhaps it is better if you struggle a little longer, if you learn to trust me with your whole heart, with all that is strong and with all that is broken inside you! See your left arm? I could heal it in an instant, but I would take away some of the strength of your character who you are and all you have been!"

Love me! Hold me, kind father! Day by day, I come here and pour out my soul to you! I offer up my thanks and praise! I spill forth my visions of hope and love!

How long, dear Father God.? How long will I sit in anguish and grief and not rise up to act and do something? How long will I languish and not lift a hand to help myself?

Time and time again you rescue and save.! Yet, I keep falling into the same pit! How long before we fill it in together or walk by a different way? Your works and your ways are not too marvelous for me! They are not so great that together we cannot accomplish them!

Let today be the turning point! Set me in motion! Cause me to rise up and act! To Go forth boldly in courage and love and peace and joy! To live fully and abundantly in you! To live generously in you! To act and to do your will! To dance and laugh and work and play!

Today is a day of feasting and of fasting! I will feast on your word! I will feast on actions of love and kindness! I will feast on the goodness and light and life and love around me! I will fast from hatred and discord, from pride and guilt and lust and greed, hatred, depression, and despair! I will feast on your word! I will feast on kindness and goodness and love! I will set captives free! I will offer hope and joy! Light and life! Go with me, kind Father and help me to follow your lead! Love me and lead me and enable and empower me to do good things!

Amen and amen! In Jesus' Name!

Bible Passages

- **Genesis 1**
- **Deuteronomy 6:4-9**
- **Joshua 1:9**
- **Psalm 1**
- **Psalm 18:1-3**
- **Psalm 27**
- **Psalm 29**
- **Psalm 30:11-12**
- **Psalm 37**
- **Psalm 46**
- **Psalm 51**
- **Psalm 73:21-28**
- **Psalm 100**
- **Psalm 103**
- **Psalm 139:8-10**
- **Psalm 143:8**
- **Psalm 145**
- **Psalm 149:1-4**
- **Proverbs 3**
- **Proverbs 11:24-25**
- **Proverbs 17:17**
- **Proverbs 31**
- **Ecclesiastes 11**
- **Isaiah 11**
- **Isaiah 25:6-9**
- **Isaiah 30:15**
- **Isaiah 43:1-3**

- **Isaiah 45:22-25**
- **Isaiah 49:15-16**
- **Isaiah 53**
- **Isaiah 60:1-3**
- **Isaiah 64:6-9**
- **Jeremiah 29:11-14**
- **Jeremiah 31:3-4**
- **Ezekiel 37**
- **Joel 2:25-26**
- **Micah 6:8**
- **Matthew 5:1-16, 43-48**
- **Matthew 6:9-15, 19-21, 25-34**
- **Matthew 7:1-12, 24-29**
- **Matthew 10:29-31, 40-42**
- **Matthew 11:28-30**
- **Matthew 15:22-28**
- **Matthew 18:2-5, 10-14, 21-35**
- **Matthew 25:35-36**
- **Matthew 28**
- **Mark 9:20-27, 35-37**
- **Mark 16:15-20**
- **Luke 6:27-49**
- **Luke 15:11-32,**
- **John 1**
- **John 3:16-17**
- **John 6**
- **John 10:10**
- **John 12:31-32**
- **John 13:34-35**
- **John 14:6-7, 27**
- **John 15:15-17**

- Acts 17:22-34
- Romans 8
- Romans 12
- 1 Corinthians 13
- 2 Corinthians 4:16-18
- Galatians 1:3-5
- Galatians 5:22-26
- Ephesians 2:8-10, 13-18
- Ephesians 3:14-21
- Ephesians 4:1-6, 15-16, 22-24
- Ephesians 5:1-2, 8-11, 15-17, 25
- Ephesians 6:10-14
- Philippians 2:5-7, 14-16
- Philippians 4:4-9
- Colossians 3:1-4
- 1 Thessalonians 1:2-5
- 1 Thessalonians 5:16-18
- Hebrews 10:24-25
- 1 Peter 1:3-4
- 1 Peter 2:9
- 1 Peter 3:15
- 1 Peter 4:8
- 1 John 1:8-2:2
- 1 John 3:1
- 1 John 4:7-12, 19-21
- Revelation 21:3-5, 22-23
- Revelation 22:1-5

Epilogue and Acknowledgements

"When you pray, you shall not be as the hypocrites, for they love to stand and pray in the synagogues and in the corners of the streets, that they may be seen by men. Most certainly, I tell you, they have received their reward. But you, when you pray, enter into your inner room, and having shut your door, pray to your Father who is in secret; and your Father who sees in secret will reward you openly. In praying, don't use vain repetitions as the Gentiles do; for they think that they will be heard for their much speaking. Therefore don't be like them, for your Father knows what things you need before you ask him. Pray like this:

"'Our Father in heaven, may your name be kept holy. Let your Kingdom come. Let your will be done on earth as it is in heaven.

Give us today our daily bread. Forgive us our debts, as we also forgive our debtors. Bring us not into temptation, but deliver us from the evil one.

For yours is the Kingdom, the power, and the glory forever. Amen.' (Matthew 6:5-13 WEB)

Even now as I put the finishing touches on this book, I have reservations about sharing it with the world, especially in light of several of the admonitions in the passage above.

These prayers were indeed originally offered in secret to my Heavenly Father in my "inner room, "a little cubbyhole of an office" in my basement and I had no intention of sharing them with anyone. Likewise, they are full of repetitions though hopefully meaningful and not vain repetitions, and my intent was certainly not to be heard for my many words. I just naturally get carried away from time to time.

So, the question remains, "Why share them with the world?" There is perhaps no simple answer. I want to, I feel God wants me to, I feel that they may be helpful to others, and I am confident that God can use them for good!

So, as I said in the introduction to this book, I offer them as "fish and bread," asking that God would use them and multiply their effect. What will that look like? I have no idea.

The book may touch the lives of many people in a profound way or one prayer, one phrase, one word may touch one person whom God then uses in a mighty way. Perhaps it will inspire someone else to begin writing and what they write will have a miraculous impact on multitudes, sparking revival throughout the nation or world. Perhaps it will but call one sinner to repentance, for which there will be much rejoicing in heaven. Perhaps it is just something I need to do to open myself up to God's continued working in my life. Perhaps it is some combination of these things or something altogether different. The results I leave in God's hands!

So, the only one I need to acknowledge is God, my loving Father, my faithful Savior, brother and friend, the indwelling Spirit of love and goodness and light! He was my constant companion in that "inner room" as

I poured out my heart day by day! It is to Him that I commend this book, asking Him to use it for His good purpose and it is into His loving and wise hands that I entrust you the reader! As His Spirit enables you, give yourself fully over to Him! You will not be disappointed!

About the Author

See how great a love the Father has given to us, that we should be called children of God!
(1 John 3:1a WEB)

"By this everyone will know that you are my disciples, if you have love for one another."
(John 13:35 WEB)

My full name is Ralph Michael Freed, but I have always been called Mike because my dad and grandpa were also named Ralph.

I am a husband; father; grandfather; uncle; great-uncle; great-great-uncle; brother; nephew; cousin; friend; retired Director of Christian Education; ex-theologian; recovering procrastinator, perfectionist, and people-pleaser; recovering emotional/binge eater; bipolar disorder and panic attack strug-gler/survivor/thriver; dreamer/schemer; jack-of-many-trades; seeker and recipient of shalom; sinner/saint; and writer. Encompassing all these things and more, I am a beloved child of God and a follower of Jesus Christ!

Sometimes incongruent, controversial, and/or clueless, I am a work in progress! My mission in life is to: "Walk Humbly and Courageously with God, Share Jesus, do Good, Love and Encourage Myself and Others!"

I'm passionate about God and people! I strive to follow two main rules in life which I learned many years ago in my work with a children's midweek program:

Rule #1: Treat everyone as a child of God!
Rule #2: See Rule #1.

I am retired, as is my wife, Linda of 43 years. I enjoy spending time with family, both immediate and extended. I work out and swim somewhat sporadically, I stay involved at church and with a few other organizations. I sometimes refurbish old laptops for a local veteran's center and for others who might not otherwise be able to afford them. When sore knees, opportunity, and weather allow it, I enjoy fishing, gardening and just generally being outdoors.

I have written two other books. Drummer Boy's Lunchbox, a smorgasbord of poems, prayers, stories, bible verses, questions, and other writings and Good Enough, a devotional journal for perfectionists, procrastinators, and other imperfect people. I have a couple other books in the works which hopefully will be out soon, including my first children's book. The plan is for Out of the Lunchbox to eventually become a series of several volumes.

I wish you all of God's manifold blessings! May He bless us and keep us, may He smile upon us and delight in us, may He enable us to grow in love, forgiveness, understanding and acceptance of ourselves and others. Peace, love and joy to you and yours!

Haven't I commanded you? Be strong and courageous. Don't be afraid. Don't be dismayed, for Yahweh your God is with you wherever you go."
(Joshua 1:9 WEB)

Made in the USA
Columbia, SC
12 February 2024

31811251R00089